MONOGRAPHS OF THE HEBREW UNION COLLEGE • NO. II

THE MESSIAH:
AN ARAMAIC INTERPRETATION

THE MESSIANIC EXEGESIS
OF THE TARGUM

THE MESSIAH:
AN ARAMAIC INTERPRETATION

THE MESSIANIC EXEGESIS
OF THE TARGUM

by

SAMSON H. LEVEY

HEBREW UNION COLLEGE-JEWISH INSTITUTE OF RELIGION
CINCINNATI, NEW YORK, LOS ANGELES, JERUSALEM
1974

Library of Congress Cataloging in Publication Data

Levey, Samson H
   The Messiah: An Aramaic Interpretation.

   (Monographs of the Hebrew Union College, no. 2)
   Based on the author's thesis, University of Southern
California
   Bibliography: p.
   1. Messianic era (Judaism) 2. Bible. O. T. Aramaic—
Criticism, interpretation, etc. I. Bible. O. T. English. Se-
lections. 1974. II. Title. III. Title: The Messianic
exegesis of the Targum. IV. Series: Hebrew Union Col-
lege-Jewish Institute of Religion. Monographs, no. 2.
BM625.L48   296.3'3   74-6239
ISBN 0-87280-402-4

MANUFACTURED IN THE UNITED STATES OF AMERICA

TABLE OF CONTENTS

Published on the
GEORGE ZEPIN
Memorial Publication Fund

FOREWORD

He is a scholar—erudite, diligent, imaginative—of whom any institution of higher learning would be proud. Only a scholar of impressive caliber would be capable of the work which Samson H. Levey has produced in the present volume.

That is not the main reason why I am so glad of the opportunity to introduce Dr. Levey's book.

He is not only a scholar. He is more—a friend and associate whom I have learned over the years to esteem and admire beyond words. He is a human being and a Jew whose values represent for me a sort of *élan vital* which I think of as exemplary for the College-Institute and for its commitment to Jewish life.

ALFRED GOTTSCHALK
President
Hebrew Union College-Jewish
Institute of Religion

PREFACE

In recent years there has been a major recognition in the field of Biblical and rabbinic scholarship of the vital importance of the Targum as an exegetical vehicle of great magnitude. The impetus in this direction is manifest by the publication of the critical edition of Alexander Sperber, *The Bible in Aramaic,* A. Diez Macho's book on the Vatican manuscript, *Neophyti I,* and J. Bowker's *The Targums and Rabbinic Literature.*

In the light of this development, the importance of a volume on "The Messianic Exegesis of the Targum" becomes immediately apparent.

The basic research for this work was contained in the author's doctoral dissertation at the University of Southern California. It was the cumulative scholarship first inspired by the great insights of my masters at the Hebrew Union College—Prof. Jacob Z. Lauterbach and Prof. Henry Englander of blessed memory; and by the profound historical methodology of Prof. Jacob R. Marcus, whose immense contributions to Jewish learning continue unabated in their impact.

I am also indebted to Prof. Willis W. Fisher, formerly head of the Department of Old Testament at the University of Southern California under whose guidance the dissertation was written; to Dr. Alfred Gottschalk, president of the Hebrew Union College-Jewish Institute of Religion who recognized the need of publishing the work, so as to bring it to the attention of the academic world; to my wife Rosalind Levey, for her encouragement; and to Miss Barbara Goldman, for her excellence in the exacting and difficult task of typing the manuscript.

Samson H. Levey
Hebrew Union College-Jewish
Institute of Religion,
Los Angeles

ט״ו בשבט   שנת כי הנני מביא את עבדי צמח

XIII

ABBREVIATIONS

The following abbreviations have been used in the course of this study:

A	Arabic translation of the Bible in Walton's Polyglott
F	Fragmentary Targum to the Pentateuch
G	Ginsburger, *Targum Pseudo-Jonathan* or Ginsburger, *Fragmententhargum, ad loc.*
H	Rendering of the Masoretic text of the Bible
J	Targum Jonathan to the Prophets
L	Lagarde, *Prophetae Chaldaice* or Lagarde, *Hagiographa Chaldaice, ad loc.*
LXX	Septuagint
MI	Messianic Implication, word or phrase in the Hebrew text from which the Targumist adduces his Messianic interpretation
N	Macho, *Neophyti 1*
O	Targum Onkelos
P	Pieterkov edition, Biblia Rabbinica
PsJ	Targum Pseudo-Jonathan to the Pentateuch
RP	Rabbinic Parallels
S	Syriac (Peshitta) version in Walton's Polyglott
SP	Sperber, *The Bible in Aramaic, ad loc.*
T	Targum
V	Vulgate
VR	Variant reading, differing from Masoretic text
W	Warsaw edition, Biblia Rabbinica

INTRODUCTION

The origin of the doctrine of the Messiah is shrouded in obscurity and is a matter of some dispute. Some contend that its earliest beginnings were not Hebraic, but that the Hebrews borrowed the idea from abroad,[1] while others maintain that it is indigenous to Israel.[2] Regardless of where it came from, the doctrine of the Messiah in its historical development is the creation of the Hebrew people.

There are sporadic references to the Messianic hope in the Hebrew Scriptures, the earliest of any significance being those of Isaiah 9:6 ff. and 11:1 ff., born of the Assyrian crisis, 721-701 B.C.E. Subsequent crises in the history of Israel such as the Exile, and the persecutions under Antiochus and Rome, gave impetus to the Messiah idea, to the point where it became a vital part of Jewish doctrine, with a prayer for the advent of the Messiah included in the daily liturgy as one of the Eighteen Benedictions,[3] whose origins go back to the third century, B.C.E., and which was redacted during the end of the first century, C.E.

The mainstream of Jewish Messianism, according to Klausner,[4] always was this-worldly and nationalistic, though the supermundane, universalistic, and individualistic lurked in the background and found open expression in the apocalyptic. Christianity, in breaking away from Judaism, emphasized these latter elements. Both Judaism and Christianity base their Messianism on the text of the Hebrew Bible. During the period of this development, two versions of the Scriptures came into being, the Septuagint and the Targum.

The present work is a critical analysis of the Messianic exegesis of the Targum, containing a detailed study of the individual passages and leading to some general conclusions concerning Targumic Messianism.

Its importance lies in the fact that such a study has not been made heretofore, although the period covered by the Targum was crucial both for Judaism and Christianity, and both lean heavily on a Messianic interpretation of history, and although the Targum constitutes a significant literary contribution in the area of Biblical translation and exegesis during this period. There are a number of relevant questions to be answered, such as the relationship of Targumic Messianic interpretation to rabbinic Messianic doctrine, on the one hand, and to Christian Messianic thought, on the other; how does Targumic interpretation compare with that of the Septuagint and that of the Vulgate and other versions with reference to the Biblical texts at issue, and is there any evidence of dependence of one version on the other in this area? These problems and others are considered as the evidence presents itself.

While there are stray references to Targumic Messianic interpretation here and there,[5] no comprehensive critical study of this theme as such, has been made before. The purpose of this volume is to provide a comprehensive, critical, analytical understanding of this neglected area.

Too much confusion has been created by loose usage of the term "Messianic,"[6] making a clear-cut definition of terminology imperative. This becomes all the more necessary in treating a theme, the rabbinic parallels of which show a tendency to lump all ideas of the Future into one, without too much discrimination or differentiation, unsystematically.[7] This laxness, if not entirely excusable, is at least understandable, in the case of the Talmud and Midrash, wherein the Biblical text is used as proof. But the subject-matter of the Targum is the Biblical text itself, something that it has in common with other translations and versions, and therefore the meaning of "Messianic" must be clearly understood. Indeed, the Targumist never did have any doubt or uncertainty as to what he meant in his interpretations; if he felt the text carried

a Messianic meaning he said so unmistakably. The following is
our delineation of Messianism as differentiated from eschatology.

Messianism is the predication of a future Golden Age in which
the central figure is a king primarily of Davidic lineage appointed
by God. In the period under consideration[8] it was believed that
during the time of the Messiah the Hebrew people will be vindi-
cated, its wrongs righted, the wicked purged from its midst, and its
rightful place in the world secured. The Messiah will pronounce
doom upon the enemies of Israel, will mete out reward and punishment in truth and in justice, and will serve as an ideal king
ruling the entire world. The Messiah may not always be the
active agent in these future events, but his personality must always
be present, at least as the symbol of the glorious age which will
be ushered in.

The eschatological is not as limited as the Messianic. It opti-
mistically envisages a salutary outcome of history, brought about
by God Himself, who will dispense reward and punishment here
and/or hereafter. Included in it are various ideas that are sometimes heterogeneous without definite plan or system. The Jewish
version usually encompasses the ingathering of the exiles and their
return to Palestine, the destruction of the armies of the archenemies
of Israel, purification of the land from defilement, the restoration
of the pristine splendor of the Temple, divine protection for
Jerusalem and its inhabitants, subjugation of the nations to God
and/or Israel, material prosperity, and peace. Attached to these
may also be the doctrine of the resurrection of the dead.[9] All this,
without the involvement of the definite personality of Davidic
lineage which marks the Messianic hope.

Interwoven into the Messianic picture may be any or all of the
eschatological elements, sometimes also some of the characteristics
of the apocalyptic, but the distinguishing feature which marks it as
such is the figure of the Messiah himself. The Targum senses this
distinction in its exegesis and mentions the Messiah without
restraint where the interpreter feels that a Messianic meaning is
present or implied in the text. The one notable exception is the
Targum to Ezekiel in which the Messiah is not designated once

as such, even though the Hebrew text itself leaves no doubt as to its Messianic intentions.[10]

Certain eschatological concepts and notions became associated with or attached to the idea of the Messiah in rabbinic thought,[11] of which the Targum is a reflection. Their occurrence in or rendition by the Targum does not make them Messianic from the exegetical standpoint unless they are accompanied by a reference to the Messiah or Messianic personality. When such reference is absent, the passage in question is eschatological but not Messianic.

The text of the Targum in the standard rabbinic Bibles bears evidence of some corruption, and, while not altogether reliable, is nevertheless important for their variant readings. Critical editions by Sperber,[12] Berliner,[13] Lagarde,[14] Ginsburger,[15] and Macho[16] were therefore used as a base, with comparative reference to two rabbinic Bibles.[17] This provided a system for checking accuracy of the text and securing the best possible reading. It also placed at our disposal the commentaries of such medieval Jewish exegetes as Rashi (France, 1040-1105), Ibn Ezra (Spain, 1093-1167), Redak (David Kimhi, Narbonne, 1160-1235), and others, all of whom are important in comparative exegesis, and especially for us, in that they sometimes quote the Targum, and not always the text which we presently have.

Inasmuch as the Targum follows the Hebrew text, and the Hebrew Scriptural order of books, we have done likewise, without rearrangement according to chronological order. The chapter and verse numbers are those of the Masoretic text, which the Targum follows.

The methodology involves the following structure of our Targumic analysis: first, there is an English translation of the original Biblical text in question, which is vital for the ready comprehension of the Targumic exegesis; followed by a translation of the Targumic Messianic rendition, in some cases an entire section rather than the mere singular reference, so as to encompass a more complete picture of the Messianic idea envisaged by the Targum. We have tried to render the translation in as readable and intelligent a manner as the Aramaic would permit. In most instances,

the circumlocutions for God which the Targum employs to soften
the anthropomorphisms in the Hebrew text have not been translated literally because of the awkwardness of such construction in
English. Throughout, the effort was made to produce an idiomatic
translation.

Following the translation there is a critical examination of the
substance of the Targumic rendering. This includes the basic
mechanics of the Targum's treatment of the Hebrew text; de-
termining the word or phrase in the text from which the Targumist
adduces his Messianic inferences; possible variant readings,
whether textual or homiletical; an appraisal of the Messianic
ideas; comparison with the other versions, if called for; rabbinic
parallels, if any; the implications of the Targumic passage; and
any other pertinent matter which can be derived from it. In the
case of the Pentateuch there is also a comparison of the three
Targumim to a given text, where this is called for.

On the strength of this detailed study and analysis, general
conclusions and evaluations are arrived at and discussed in the
fourth chapter.

Finally, the Appendix provides a list of those passages in the
Targum which contain literal translations of the Hebrew text where
the word *Mashiah* occurs, in the simple sense of an anointed one,
without Messianic connotation.

CHAPTER I

THE MESSIANIC EXEGESIS OF THE
TARGUMIM TO THE PENTATEUCH

Three Targumic sources to the Pentateuch have been used:
(1) Targum Onkelos, abbreviated O, which was the official Targum used in the synagogue service, and which is complete, covering every verse in the Pentateuch in a fairly literal rendering.
(2) Targum Pseudo-Jonathan, abbreviated PsJ, which bears the
name of Jonathan b. Uzziel, on the strength of Jonathan's authority
as the official Targum to the Prophets, but which was actually
pseudonymous and had no official stamp of approval; it is a complete Targum and much fuller than O, containing a great deal of
Aggadic material. (3) The Fragmentary Targum, abbreviated F,
which is designated as "Yerushalmi," the Jerusalem Targum, in
the Rabbinic Bibles. It contains only certain fragments, as if in
explanation of some other Targum. Like Pseudo-Jonathan, it had
no official approval, and its content is largely Aggadic. The critical
editions of Sperber and Berliner on Onkelos, and Ginsburger on
Pseudo-Jonathan and the Fragmentary as well as Macho were
compared with the Targumic texts found in the Pieterkov and
Warsaw editions of the rabbinic Pentateuch. Our rendering of the
Hebrew text follows the Masoretic reading.

1

GENESIS

H   3:15   And I will put enmity between you and the woman, and between your seed and her seed; he will strike your head and you will strike his heel.

PsJ   3:15   I will put enmity between you and the woman, and between the offspring of your sons and the offspring of her sons; and it shall be that when the sons of the woman observe the commandments of the Torah, they will direct themselves[1] to smite you on the head, but when they forsake the commandments of the Torah you will direct yourself[1] to bite them on the heel. However, there is a remedy for them, but no remedy for you. They are destined to make peace in the end, in the days of the King Messiah.

F   3:15   And it shall be that when the sons of the woman study the Torah diligently and obey its injunctions, they will direct themselves[1] to smite you on the head and slay you; but when the sons of the woman forsake the commandments of the Torah and do not obey its injunctions, you will direct yourself[1] to bite them on the heel and afflict them. However, there will be a remedy for the sons of the woman, but for you, serpent, there will be no remedy. They shall make peace with one another in the end, in the very end of days, in the days of the King Messiah.

PsJ and F are essentially the same, with a somewhat fuller exposition by the latter. The interpretation is allegorical. Enmity between woman and serpent represents the struggle between good and evil tendencies in man, with the serpent symbolic of evil. Torah enables man to strike down the evil impulse, but its absence leaves man a prey to it.[2] The "remedy" is Torah, the antidote which will come into its own when the Messiah comes. F also implies that there will be reconciliation between man and serpent.

MI: עָקֵב which T read עֵקֶב, "ultimate end." Also play on words from תְּשׁוּפֶנּוּ , "you shall bruise," to Aramaic שפיותא , "peace," "tranquility."

RP: "R. Levi said: In the Messianic age all will be healed save the serpent and the Gibeonite." Genesis Rabbah 20:5. On the reconciliation of serpent and man, there are no rabbinic parallels, but there does seem to be some connection with Is. 11:8.

The other versions of this passage give no specific Messianic interpretation, yet Christianity regarded it as the Protoevangelium.[3] In the Targumic interpretation there is no hint of original sin, but the Targum's influence on Christian Messianic thought on' this passage is unmistakable.

Gen.

H   35:21   And Israel journeyed on, pitching his tent from there to Migdal-Eder.

PsJ   And Jacob moved on, and pitched his tent onward to the tower of Eder, the place whence the King Messiah is destined to reveal himself at the end of days.[4]

MI: מִגְדַּל עֵדֶר מִגְדַּל "the tower," and עֵדֶר , "the flock," Israel. Compare Mic. 4:8, where, in a definitely Messianic context in the Hebrew, J renders "And you, O tower of Eder" as "And you, O Messiah of Israel."

The Hebrew מֵהָלְאָה, "from there," is taken in the sense of time, rather than of place.

PsJ sees in this verse a reflection of the history of the Jew, and from his standpoint it could be translated: "And Israel wandered on, pitching his tent, thenceforth until the coming of the Messiah." The coming of the Messiah will end Israel's wandering.

Gen.

H   49:1   And Jacob called to his sons and said, "Gather together, and I will relate to you what will happen to you at the end of days."

PsJ   49:1   Then Jacob called his sons and said to them: "Purify yourselves of uncleanness, and I will tell you the hidden secrets, the concealed date of the End,[5] the reward of the righteous and the punishment of the wicked, and what the pleasure of Paradise will be." The twelve sons[6] of Israel gathered together around the golden bed on which he lay. As soon as the date of the End[7] when the King Messiah would arrive was revealed to him, it was immediately concealed from him;[8] and therefore, instead (of revealing the date) he said: "Come, and I will relate to you what will happen to you at the end of days."

F   49:1   Then Jacob called his sons and said to them: "Gather together and I will tell you what will happen to you, about the rewarding of the righteous and the punishment destined for the wicked at the time when you are gathered together again at the end of days." For he was revealing to them all that was going to occur at the very end, the time of the Messiah.[9] But as soon as it was revealed to him it became concealed from him. So Jacob arose and blessed them, each according to his deserts.[10]

MI: בְּאַחֲרִית הַיָמִים , "at the end of days." The Targumists see here the psychological moment to discourage speculation about the exact date of the advent of the Messiah. If Jacob was forbidden to do so in this situation, it stands to reason that no one has permission to speculate.

Messianic speculation and calculation were widespread immediately following the destruction of the Temple in 70 C.E.[11] The period naturally lent itself to Messianic expectation, culminating in the disaster which befell the Jews when the most promising Messianic prospect,[12] Bar Kokhba, was crushed by Rome, and very many Jews with him. R. Akiba had pinned his Messianic hopes on this military leader, and, when it became apparent that even the great rabbi had erred, reaction set in against speculation and calculation.[13] This is reflected in our Targum, as well as in the Tannaitic sources, in statements such as "Seven things are concealed from man . . . when the Davidic dynasty will be restored and when the guilty kingdom (Rome) will fall," [14] "may their bones be crushed, who calculate ends," [15] and "he who specifies the date of the End has no share in the World-to-Come." [16]

The reference to purification in PsJ signifies that what was about to be revealed was regarded as sacred, and one had to be ritually pure even to hear it.

RP: "Purify yourselves." "R. Phineas the priest, son of Hama, and R. Judah the Levite,[17] son of R. Shalom, said: What is the meaning of הֵאָסְפוּ ? 'Purify yourselves,' as in the verse, 'Let her be shut up without the camp seven days and after that she shall be purified—תֵּאָסֵף,' (Num. 12:14)." Genesis Rabbah, N.V., 96, and 98:2.

The attempted revelation of the date of the advent of the Messiah by Jacob, and its sudden withdrawal are discussed in Genesis Rabbah 98:2.

Gen.

H 49:10 The scepter shall not depart from Judah, nor the staff of law from between his feet until Shiloh comes. And unto him shall be the obedience of the peoples.

O The transmission of dominion[18] shall not cease from the house of Judah, nor the scribe from his children's children, forever, until the Messiah comes, to whom the Kingdom belongs, and whom nations shall obey.

H 49:11 He binds his foal to the vine, his colt to the choice vine; he washes his garment in wine, and his robe in the blood of grapes.

O He shall enclose Israel in his city, the people shall build his Temple, the righteous shall surround him, and those who serve the Torah by teaching shall be with him. His raiment shall be of goodly purple, and his garment of the finest brightly-dyed wool.[19]

H 49:12 His eyes shall be red with wine and his teeth white with milk.

O His mountains shall be red with his vineyards, his vats[20] shall drip with wine; his valleys shall be white with corn and with flocks of sheep.

The Targumist takes the passage as a metaphor and proceeds to explain it in more simplified language.

VR: While there are a number of language twists for homiletical-exegetical purposes here, there may be a genuine textual variant in v. 10, שֵׁלֹה, for שִׁילֹה .

MI: A combination of שֵׁבֶט and שִׁילֹה .

In v. 10, the scepter represents dominion, and מְחֹקֵק not law-giver, but he who studies the חֻקִּים, "scribe." In v. 11, אֹסְרִי from אָסַר, "to enclose protectively;" "vine" is Israel; the Masoretic *Q're,* עִירוֹ , "his city," Jerusalem. "The choice vine" refers to the people; בְּנִי , T takes from בָּנָה , "to build;" אֲתֹנוֹ from אֵיתָן , "strength," "spiritual power," hence "Temple." The righteous and those who teach Torah—a paraphrastic insert referring back to the scribe in v. 10. The color and quality of the garments refer to the vesture of Messianic royalty.

Verse 12 is paraphrastic of the Hebrew text which O takes as metaphor.

The Messianic picture which O paints contains the restoration of the Davidic dynasty, implied in the context of Judah, the Messiah's dominion over the nations, divine protection for Jerusalem and its inhabitants, the rebuilding of the sanctuary, the prevalence of righteousness and the ideal of Torah and education,[21] and material prosperity. The picture is one of peacefulness, tranquility, culture and refinement. It reflects a secure state of mind, with no thought of vengeance or bloodshed.

LXX: Verse 10, ". . . until there come the things stored up for him, and he is the expectation of the nations."

V: ". . . until he comes who is to be sent." [22]

S: ". . . until he comes to whom it is." S follows O in reading שֶׁלֹּה . RSV does likewise.

RP: Other rabbinic sources, both Midrashic and Talmudic, also take this passage as Messianic, but practically none handles the words and phrases in their specific connotation as does O, with one exception: "Until Shiloh comes: he to whom kingship belongs (שֶׁלֹּה)." Genesis Rabbah 98:8. Compare the rest of this section, as well as 98:8-10 for specific differences in interpretation. Also Sanhedrin 98b: 'What is his (Messiah's) name? The school of R. Shila said, 'Shiloh' [23] as it is written, until Shiloh come."

Gen.

PsJ 49:10   Kings and rulers shall not cease from the house of Judah, nor scribes who teach the Torah from his seed, until the time when the King Messiah shall come, the youngest of his sons, and because of him nations shall melt away.

11   How beautiful is the King Messiah who is destined to arise from the house of Judah! He has girded his loins and gone down to battle against his enemies, destroying kings and their power, and there is neither king nor power that can withstand him. He reddens the mountains with the blood of their slain. His garments are saturated with blood, like those of him who presses the grapes.[24]

12   How beautiful are the eyes of the King Messiah, as pure wine! He will not see incestuous practice or the shedding of innocent blood. And his teeth are more pure than milk, for he will not tolerate as food that which is seized by force or taken by robbery.[25]

PsJ is freer, more paraphrastic than O. He accepts the Masoretic reading, שִׁילֹה, and interprets it in the sense of שִׁיל, "embryo," hence "young" or "youngest." Compare Dt. 28:57, וּבְשִׁלְיָתָה, which Rashi, following O *ad loc.*, renders "young sons." Reference to the Messiah as the youngest son of Judah has no RP. It may point to the Messiah as the last, hence youngest, in the line of Davidic succession; or, it may be a reference to David, the founder of the dynasty, the youngest of the sons of Jesse, I Sam. 16:10 ff. The idea of his beauty and beautiful eyes may likewise reflect the description of David in I Sam. 16:12. The bloody allusions in v. 11 are a reflection of Is. 63:1-6, and are apocalyptic. Cf. Rev. 19:11-15.

The Messianism in PsJ is a combination of overwhelming military might which exacts bloody vengeance from the enemies of Israel,[26] and personal as well as national righteousness marked by the elimination of the three cardinal transgressions—idolatry, incest, and murder,[27] the first of these implied and the latter two expressed explicitly; also the rectification of social injustices, such as seizure by force, robbery, violence. Prosperity[28] is the reward of good conduct.

Two things are especially worthy of note. One, PsJ's interpretation of v. 11b as metaphor, providing the most sanguinary portrait imaginable.[29] Secondly, his usage of the participial form throughout this passage, which in Targumic Aramaic, tends to make it a definite present. There is a very strong likelihood that this stems from an occurring historical event to which the Targumist was an eyewitness, and such an event most probably was the ascendancy of Bar Kokhba in his revolt against Rome.

There is a close resemblance between PsJ on v. 12 and V, which reads: "His eyes are more beautiful than wine, etc." Jerome's acquaintance with, reliance on and utilization of Jewish sources is well known,[30] and this is just one more demonstration of the fact.

Gen.

F   49:10   Kings shall not cease from the house of Judah, nor scribes[31] who teach the Torah from his children's children, until the time of the coming of the King Messiah, to whom belongs the Kingdom, and to whom all dominions of the earth shall become subservient.

        11   How beautiful is he, the King Messiah, who is destined to arise from the house of Judah. He has girded his loins and gone forth to battle against his enemies, slaying kings[32] and[33] rulers, and making the mountains[34] red with the blood of their slain and the hills white with the fat of their mighty ones. His garments are saturated[35] with blood, and he is like the treader of grapes.[36]

        12   How beautiful to behold are they, the eyes of the King Messiah, more so than pure wine, not looking upon incest and the shedding of innocent blood. His teeth are pure, according to the Halakah, refraining from partaking of that which is taken by violence or robbery. His mountains shall be red with vines, his presses with wine. His hills shall be white with the abundance of his grain and flocks of his sheep.

F is essentially the same as PsJ, though it departs from PsJ and agrees with O in reading שִׁלֹה in v. 10. In v. 11 there is a variation in the sanguinary nature of the Messianic war, with the additional picture of the hills being white with the fat of the mighty ones. In v. 12, F introduces the element of Halakah, by which the Messiah will abide, bolstering the contention that both PsJ and F to these Biblical verses are contemporary with the Bar Kokhba revolt, since the edict of Hadrian had suppressed the Halakah,[37] and the study of the Torah, both of which the Messiah will restore.

EXODUS

H   12:42   It was a night of watching for the Lord, to bring them out of the land of Egypt. This same night for the Lord is one of watching for all the children of Israel throughout their generations.

F   It is a night of waiting, appointed for deliverance by the Lord, when the children of Israel were brought forth liberated from the land of Egypt. There are four nights recorded in the Book of Memorials:

The first night, when the Memra of the Lord was revealed to the world in order to create it. The world was desolate and void and darkness spread over the face of the abyss and the Memra of the Lord was bright and illuminating; and He called it the first night.

The second night was when the Memra of the Lord was revealed to Abraham between the pieces. Abraham was one hundred years old and Sarah was ninety years old, to fulfill what Scripture says, "Is it possible for Abraham at age one hundred to sire a child, and is it possible for Sarah, at age ninety, to give birth to a child?" Was not our Father Isaac thirty seven years old at the time that he was offered on the altar. The heavens bent and came down, and Isaac saw their perfection and his eyes were weakened because of the heights. He called this the second night.

The third night, when the Memra of the Lord revealed itself against the Egyptians at midnight, His hand[38] slaying the first born of the Egyptians and His right hand sparing the firstborn of Israel to fulfill what Scripture says, "My son, my firstborn, these are Israel." And this He called the third night.

The fourth night, when the world shall have completed its allotted time until the End,[39] when it should be delivered, when the bands of wickedness shall be destroyed and the iron yoke broken. Moses shall go forth from the wilderness and the King Messiah from Rome. The one shall lead the way on top of a cloud and the other shall lead the way on top of a cloud, and the Memra of the Lord shall lead the way between the two of them, and they shall proceed togcthcr. This is the night of the Passover of the Lord, awaited and appointed for all Israel throughout their generations.

MI: לְדֹרֹתָם, "throughout their generations," implying the very end of time, the time of the Messiah.

The linking together of Moses and the Messiah is striking, carrying the force of historical determination, the final drama of Israel's history to be a re-enactment of the deliverance which marked the beginning of Israel's career as a nation. Compare the parallels in the lives of Moses and Jesus implied in the Synoptics, such as being hidden in the basket and in the manger (Luke 2:7); the threat of Pharoah and the threat of Herod (Matt. 2:13); flight to Egypt and return of Jesus (Matt. 2:13 ff.); the forty days of seclusion (Mark 1:13); the Torah handed down from the mountain and the Sermon on the Mount (Matt. 5:1 ff.), etc. The Targumic use of the imperfect tense in the case of Moses is startling, but the Targumist obviously expects a return of Moses to participate in the Messianic deliverance, with the Messiah, Moses and the Memra forming a trio, leading the way on the clouds. The resurrection of the dead, which came to be linked with Messianism, makes this possible. There is an interesting comparison with Mark 9:4 ff., in which Moses, Elijah and Jesus constitute a trio, and the voice of God speaks from a cloud.[40]

The Book of Memorials may be a literary device to indicate a very significant event or it may be a mystic allusion to the heavenly record. PsJ calls it "The Book of Memorials of the Lord." The other two nights referred to are Creation and the revelation to Abram, stated explicitly in this same passage in the Targum.

The Messiah's coming from Rome, RP: R. Joshua b. Levi found the Messiah sitting at the gate of Rome among the poor and the sick, Sanhedrin 98a.

Moses leading the way on a cloud, possibly a reference to Exod. 13:21. The Messiah coming on a cloud, reference to Dan. 7:13, discussed in Sanhedrin 98a: "If they (Israel) are meritorious, (he will come) on the clouds of heaven, etc."

RP: ". . . and that night (the anniversary of the event in Egypt), the Messiah and Elijah will appear," Exodus Rabbah 18:12.

Exod.

H 17:16   And he said, "Verily, a hand upon the throne of the Lord! The Lord will be at war with Amalek from generation to generation."

PsJ   And he said: The Memra of the Lord has sworn by His throne of glory that He would wage war against Amalek's house through the instrumentality of His Memra, and would destroy them from three generations—from the generation of this world, and from the generation of the Messiah,[41] and from the generation of the World-to-Come.

MI: מִדֹּר דֹּר , "from generation to generation," i.e., each important era, this age, the age of the Messiah, and the World-to-Come. Note the definite distinction between the latter two. Amalek, the historical enemy of Israel, will again turn up as an adversary in the Messianic age, and will be destroyed, not by the Messiah, but by the Memra. The hand on the throne is understood as an oath.

RP: R. Joshua says, "from generation"—this refers to the life of this world; "to generation," this refers to the life of the world to come. "From generation to generation . . . R. Eliezer said: From the generation of the Messiah, which comprises three generations, and whence do we deduce that the generation of the Messiah comprises three generations? As it is said (Ps. 72:5), they shall fear thee with the sun, and as long as the moon, generation after generation." Mekilta, Amalek, II, *ad loc.*

Exod.

H   40:9   And you shall take the anointing oil and anoint the tabernacle and all that is in it and you shall consecrate it and
all of its appurtenances and it shall be sacred.

PsJ   Then you shall take the anointing oil and anoint the tabernacle and all that is in it, and consecrate it for the crown
of the kingdom of the house of Judah and the King Messiah, who is destined to redeem Israel at the end of days.

H   40:10   And you shall anoint the altar of the burnt-offering and all
its appurtenances and the altar shall be Holy of Holies.

PsJ   And you shall anoint the sacrificial altar and all its vessels,
and consecrate it as an altar of the Holy of Holies, for the
crown of the priesthood of Aaron and his sons, and of
Elijah the High Priest, who is to be sent at the end of the
Dispersions.

H   40:11   And you shall anoint the laver and its base and consecrate
it.

PsJ   And you shall anoint the laver and its base, and consecrate
it for Joshua your servant, chief of the Sanhedrin of his
people, by whose hand the land of Israel is to be divided,
and from whom is to descend the Messiah son of Ephraim,
by whose hand the house of Israel is to vanquish Gog and
his confederates at the end of days.[42]

MI: שֶׁמֶן הַמִּשְׁחָה , "anointing oil."

The threefold use of the expression, "and you shall anoint," and
the objects to be anointed, indicate the three central personalities
of the Messianic drama. The tabernacle represents the Davidic
line, builders of the Temple; the altar represents priesthood, identified as Elijah; the laver and base represent the more menial, the
servant Joshua the Ephraimite, and his descendant, the Messiah
son of Ephraim.

In rabbinic thought Elijah comes to be identified as Phineas
the son of Aaron and is frequently referred to as the High Priest
of the Messianic age,[43] the precursor of the Messiah (Mal. 3:23),

the religious counterpart of the political figure. Elijah would restore, among other things, the vial of anointing oil.[44] Subsequently it was thought that he would also anoint the Messiah.[45]

The Ephraimite Messiah does not figure too prominently or clearly in rabbinic thought. Such a personality was probably built up as a psychological reaction to the death of Bar Kokhba; he will be a conquering hero who will actually lead in the final battle, and will be slain and mourned.[46] The implication of PsJ is that the Ephraimite Messiah will do the fighting and vanquish Gog, while the Davidic King Messiah will be the symbol of deliverance. Rabbinic sources do not indicate the reason why this personality is depicted as of Ephraimite descent, but it may be conjectured that this represents that phase of the Messianic hope in which a reunion of the Northern and Southern Kingdoms was expected.

In the Babylonian Talmud the Ephraimite Messiah is referred to only once, in the context of Sukkah 52a-b, where he is designated as the Messiah, son of Joseph. There is also a possible allusion in Gen. R. 75:6. The exact title that we have here is used in the medieval apocalypse, *Sefer Zerubabel*. Compare also, the Targum to Song of Songs 4:5 and 7:4, *infra,* pp. 127-128.

NUMBERS

H 11:26   And there remained two men in the camp, the name of
one was Eldad, and the name of the second one was Medad.
And the spirit rested upon them. They were of those who
had been recorded, but they had not gone out to the tent.
So they prophesied in the camp.

F   Two men remained in the camp, the name of the one
Eldad and the name of the other Medad, and the Holy
Spirit rested upon them . . . and the two of them prophesied
together, saying: "At the end, the very end of days Gog
and Magog and their armies shall go up against Jerusalem,
but they shall fall by the hand of the King Messiah. For
seven full years the children of Israel shall use their (Gog's,
etc.) weapons of war for kindling, without having to go
into the forest to cut down the trees."

This is an excellent example of the exegetical complement.
Scripture does not relate the contents of the Eldad and Medad
prophecy; hence the Targumist fills it in. There is no specific MI
in the text. Reference to the kindling is taken from the Gog passage, Ezek. 39:9-10.

Note that the King Messiah is here depicted as the active agent
in the destruction of Gog and Magog, unlike PsJ in the passage
cited above, where the Ephraimite Messiah is the active agent.

RP: "What did they (Eldad and Medad) prophesy? Some say:
the downfall of Gog, etc." Numbers Rabbah, 15:19.

PsJ on this verse, eschatological but not Messianic, is interesting:

. . . together the two of them prophesied and said: "Behold, a
king shall go up from the land of Magog at the end of days. He
shall assemble kings wearing crowns and lieutenants wearing ar-
mour, and all the nations shall obey him. They shall array battle
in the land of Israel against the children of the Dispersion, but the
Lord[47] shall be ready for them by burning the breath of life out
of them with the flame of fire that issues from beneath the throne
of glory.[48] Their dead bodies shall fall upon the mountains of the

land of Israel, and the wild beasts of the field and the birds of heaven shall come and consume them. After that, all the dead of Israel shall be resurrected, and shall enjoy the good things which were secretly set aside for them from the beginning, and they shall receive the reward of their labor."

The active agent is God. The manner in which God slays them is the same that destroyed Nadab and Abihu (Lev. 10:1 f.); according to rabbinic tradition, the breath of life was burned out of them while the body remained intact.[49] PsJ also draws on the Gog passage in Ezekiel, 39:4 f.

Num.

H   23:21   He has not beheld iniquity in Jacob, nor has he seen per-
verseness in Israel. The Lord his God is with him, and the
shouting of the king is in him.

PsJ   Balaam the wicked said: "I do not observe any idol-wor-
shippers among the house of Jacob, and those who serve
false gods are not established in the house of Israel. The
Memra of the Lord their God is their help, and the trumpet-
call of the King Messiah echoes in their midst."

MI: וּתְרוּעַת מֶלֶךְ , "and the *terua* of the king." "Terua" is a
reference to the blowing of the Shofar. Both O and F take it as
referring to God; O: "Shekinah of their King;" F: "glory of their
King."

LXX: "glories of rulers."

V: "sound of victory of the king," which follows our Targum.

S: "glory of his king."

The idea of a Messianic trumpet, שופרו של משיח , is based on
Is. 27:13 and Zech. 9:14, but it is the trumpet of the Messianic
age, blown not by the Messiah himself but by God, the trumpet-
call being the signal of deliverance.

RP: "Said R. Judan: After all that happened, Israel still falls
into the clutches of sin and becomes the victim of persecution; yet
they will be ultimately redeemed by the ram's horn . . . R. Abba b.
Pappi and R. Joshua of Siknin in R. Levi's name said: Because
the Patriarch Abraham saw the ram extricate itself from one
thicket and become entangled in another, the Holy One, blessed
be He, said to him: 'So will your children be entangled in countries,
changing from Babylon to Media, from Media to Greece, and
from Greece to Edom (Rome); yet they will eventually be redeemed by the ram's horn,' as it is written, And the Lord God
will blow the horn, etc.[50] Who will blow the horn? Scripture
teaches, And the Lord God will blow the horn, etc." [51]

"Said R. Hanina b. Dosa: That ram which Abraham offered up
in place of his son Isaac, nothing of it went to waste . . . the left
horn was the trumpet of Sinai and the right horn the trumpet of
the Messianic Future." [52]

Num.

H   24:7   Water shall flow from his buckets and his seed shall be in many waters; and his king shall be more exalted than Agag and his kingdom shall be lifted on high.

F   Their king shall arise from among them, and their deliverer shall be of them and with them. He shall gather in their exiles from the provinces of their enemies, and their sons shall have dominion over the nations. He shall be mightier than Saul, who spared Agag, king of the Amalekites. Exalted shall be the kingdom of the King Messiah.

MI: מַיִם , "water," interpreted as Messiah. Compare John 7:37 f., where Jesus refers to himself and the Spirit as water. מֵאֲגַג , "from Agag," F takes not as referring to Agag proper, but to the king who conquered Agag, namely, Saul.

VR: בְּעַמִּים , "among nations," instead of בְּמַיִם , "in water," in second part of 7a.

Both O and PsJ interpret this passage historically, not Messianically, as referring to Saul, who was removed from the kingdom of Israel because he violated divine injunction by sparing Agag (1 Sam. 15:8 ff).

LXX: "There shall come a man out of his seed, and he shall rule over many nations; and the kingdom of God shall be exalted, and his kingdom shall be increased." Not necessarily Messianic. The LXX passage is difficult as it stands.

S: "A man shall come out of his sons and his seed shall be in many waters; and he shall be exalted over King Agag, but his kingdom shall be removed." Follows O and refers to Saul, but is not Messianic.

V: Literal.

There is no RP for this Messianic interpretation.

Num.

H 24:17   I see him, but not now, I behold him but not near; a star
shall step forth out of Jacob, and a scepter shall arise out
of Israel, and shall crush the corners of Moab, and break
down all the sons of Seth.

O   "I see him, but not now; I behold him, but he is not near;
when a king shall arise out of Jacob and be anointed the
Messiah out of Israel.[53] He shall slay the princes of Moab
and reign over all mankind.

H 24:18   And Edom shall be an inheritance, and an inheritance, too,
Seir, his enemies; but Israel shall do valiantly.

O   Edom shall become an inheritance and Seir shall become
a possession of its enemies, but Israel shall prosper in
wealth.

H 24:19   And he shall have dominion from Jacob and shall destroy
the remnant from the city.

O   One shall descend from the house of Jacob who will destroy any survivor of the city of the nations."

H 24:20   And he saw Amalek, and he took up his parable and said:
Amalek was the first of the nations, but his end shall come
to destruction.

O   He saw the Amalekite, and took up his parable and said:
"Amalek was the first to make war on Israel, and his end
shall be that he shall be destroyed forever."

H 24:21   And he saw the Kenite and he took up his parable and
said: Firm is your dwelling place and your nest is set in
the rock.

O   He saw the Shalmaite and took up his parable and said:
"Strong is the house in which you dwell, and he has placed
your abode in a fortified city.

H 24:22   Nevertheless Kain shall become a waste; how long? Asshur
shall take you captive.

O   However, when shall the Shalmaite be for destruction?
When the Assyrian will take you captive."

H   24:23   And he took up his parable and said: Alas, who shall live unless God had appointed him?

O   And he took up his parable and said: "Woe unto the guilty who live when God shall do these things.

H   24:24   For ships shall come from the coast of Kittim. And they shall afflict Eber. And he, too, shall come to destruction.

O   And troops mustered by the Romans shall afflict Assyria, and shall subjugate those beyond the Euphrates, and they also shall be destroyed forever."

MI: כּוֹכָב , "star," and שֵׁבֶט, "scepter," v. 17.

In v. 17, Seth, son of Adam, is regarded as progenitor of all mankind, and is interpreted as all mankind by O. In v. 18, חָיִל, is understood as "wealth" rather than "military might," contrasting Israel with Edom, which shall be despoiled. Edom and Amalek are related (Gen. 36:16). In rabbinic thought they represent Rome.[54] Verse 19, מֵעִיר , which O understands as "from *the* city," Rome, as indicated in v. 24. Verse 20, Amalek, the archenemy of Israel, will have a role in the final drama as at the beginning of Israel's history. Verse 23, the guilty can be none other than the Romans.   וְצִים מִיַּד כִּתִּים is taken as Roman soldiers; in Dan. 11:30 it refers to ships from Greece, but O saw the Romans as successors to Greece, and interprets צִים as soldiers because they are transported in galleys. עֵבֶר , those on the other side (of the Euphrates). Assyria, the first power to threaten Israel with annihilation, shall be punished by Rome. All the great military nations, enemies of Israel, shall meet doom in the end.

The star out of Jacob as the Messiah gained prominence in Jewish thought, in the time of Bar Kokhba, to whom R. Akiba applied the name on the basis of this passage in Scripture.[55] It also found expression in Christian exegesis, Matt. 2:2.

The main emphasis of O is the destruction of Rome, its utter annihilation down to the last man. The Messiah is a military figure performing relatively moderate deeds of valor, who becomes the ruler of the entire world.

Num.
PsJ 24:17   "I see him, but he is not at the present time, I behold him but he is not near; but when a mighty king of the house of Jacob shall reign, and shall be anointed Messiah,[56] wielding the mighty scepter of Israel. He shall slay the Moabite princes and shall bring to naught all the sons of Seth, the armies of Gog, destined to wage war against Israel, and their dead bodies shall fall before him.

18   And the Edomites shall be driven out, and the sons of Gabla shall be banished before Israel, their foes, but Israel shall become rich and possess them.

19   A ruler shall arise from the house of Jacob who shall utterly destroy the remnant escaping from Constantinople,[57] the guilty city, and completely demolish the sinful city of Caesarea, the mighty city of the Gentiles."

20   He saw the house of Amalek, and he took up the parable of his prophecy and said: "The house of Amalek was the first nation to wage war against Israel, and they shall be the last ones, together with all the sons of the East, to wage war against Israel, in the days of the King Messiah. But ultimately all of them shall suffer eternal destruction."

21   And he saw Jethro that he had become a proselyte to Judaism, and he took up his prophetic parable and said, "How mighty it is, your camp, in that you have set your abode in the clefts of the rocks.

22   Verily, if the sons of the Shalmaites are decreed to be despoiled, it will be when Sennacherib, King of Assyria, shall come and take you captive."

23   And he took up the parable of his prophecy and said: "Woe unto him who is alive when the Memra of the Lord reveals itself, rewarding the righteous and punishing the wicked, smiting nations and kings, and thrusting one against the other.

24   Troops[58] ready for battle, with great armed might, shall go forth from Italy in Liburnian ships, joining the legions

which shall go forth from Rome[59] and Constantinople. They
shall afflict the Assyrians and subjugate all the sons of
Eber. However, the end of both these and those shall be
to fall by the hand of the King Messiah and be destroyed
forever."

PsJ introduces the war of Gog, in which the Messiah will be
victorious, an eschatological element which O does not mention.
There are also references to Constantinople, Caesarea, and Gabla,
and Liburnian ships sallying forth from Italy carrying Roman
soldiers. The Messianism is more drastic than that of O.

Num.

F   24:17   "I see him, but he is not here now, I behold him, but he
is not near. A king is destined to arise from the house of
Jacob, a redeemer and ruler from the house of Israel, who
shall slay the mighty ones of the Moabites, who shall bring
to naught[60] all the sons of the East.

18   Edom shall be inherited, and Mt. Gabla shall be possessed
by its enemies, but Israel shall become stronger in armed
might.[61]

19   A king is destined to arise from the house of Jacob who
shall destroy all that remains of the guilty city, which is
Rome." [62]

20   He beheld the Amalekite and took up the parable of his
prophecy, and said: "The first nation to set up war against
Israel were they of the house of Amalek, and at the very
end of time they shall again array battle against them; but
their end shall be destruction, and their destruction shall be
final."

21   And he saw the Shalmaites and he took up his prophecy
by way of parable and said, "How mighty is your camp,
you have set the house of your dwelling place in the cleft
of the rock.

22   Verily, if the Shalmaites shall be for a spoil, it shall be
until the time that the Assyrians arise to capture you."

23   "Woe unto the guilty[63] when God comes to punish the
wicked and reward the righteous, and when He thrusts the
kingdoms of the nations one against the other.

24   Great armies shall go forth in Liburnian ships[64] from Italy,
which is Rome,[65] and shall join many Roman legions, that
shall subjugate the Assyrians and afflict all the people beyond the River. But destruction shall befall both these and
those, an everlasting destruction."

Though there is no specific mention of the Messiah in F, the contents are similar to O and PsJ, but are not obviously Messianic, but eschatological. This is an excellent example of the difference. It also points up the fact that the various Targumim are at times remarkably independent in their Messianic understanding and interpretations of the Biblical text. Even the Septuagint, which is generally literal in its rendition of Scriptures and extremely cautious about reading a specific Messianic meaning into the Hebrew, has strong Messianic overtones in its translation of this passage, which is regarded by many as a pericope of Pentateuchal poetry serving as a Scriptural Messianic prototype.

O, who is also circumspect in his Messianism, is articulately Messianic at this point. Why F would choose to ignore the Messianic potential in v. 17, and does not designate the title of the Messiah to the king whom he sees in the passage is puzzling. The thrust and the language, as well as the historical references are decidedly Messianic in tone, yet F stops short of a definitive Messianic exposition.

We know so little about the origins and development of F that it would be useless to speculate or venture a conjecture on the subject. This is especially true in view of F's unquestionable Messianic interpretations elsewhere in the Pentateuch. This would also preclude any considerations such as we have put forth with reference to J's rendering of Ezekiel, in our discussion of that Targum.

LXX: "I will point to him but not now. I bless him, but he draws not near. A star shall rise out of Jacob, a man shall spring out of Israel and shall crush the princes of Moab and shall spoil all the sons of Seth. And Edom shall be an inheritance, and Israel wrought valiantly. And· one shall arise out of Jacob, and destroy out of the city him that escapes. And having seen Amalek, he took up his parable and said: Amalek is the first of the nations, yet his seed shall perish . . . And one shall come forth from the lands of the Citians and shall afflict the[66] Hebrews, etc."

V: Likewise Messianic. Note the similarity to PsJ and F in v. 24: "They shall come in galleys from Italy; they shall overcome the Assyrians and waste the Hebrews,[66] etc."

S: Understands צִים , in v. 24, as "legions."

DEUTERONOMY

H   25:19   And it shall come to pass, when the Lord your God gives
you rest from all your enemies around you, in the land
which the Lord your God is giving you as an inheritance
to possess it, you must blot out the memory of Amalek
from under the heavens; you must not forget.

PsJ   And it shall come to pass, when the Lord your God shall
have given you rest from all the enemies which surround
you, in the land which the Lord your God gives you as
possession to inherit, you shall blot out the memory of
Amalek from under heaven. Even unto the days of the
King Messiah, you shall not forget.

MI: לֹא תִּשְׁכָּח, "you must not forget," ever, unto the remotest
future.

The complete destruction of Amalek will be achieved by God,
according to the Targumist, who visualizes God as taking an oath
to that effect.[67] Israel is to follow suit by erasing the memory of
his enemy, putting him completely out of his mind and his heart;
he is not to have any thoughts, feelings, or emotions about him.[68]
This injunction is to apply down to the days of the Messiah, for
in those days Israel will achieve final victory over Amalek, or
Esau, or Rome, all of whom are identical in rabbinic thinking.

Dt.

H 30:4 Even if your dispersed ones are at the ends of heaven, from there the Lord your God will gather you, and from there He will take you.

PsJ If your dispersed ones will be unto the end of heaven, from there the Memra of the Lord your God shall gather you by the hand of Elijah, the High Priest, and from there He shall bring you near by the hand of the King Messiah.

H 30:5 And the Lord your God will bring you to the land which your fathers possessed, and you will possess it; and He will be better to you and make you more numerous than your fathers.

PsJ And the Memra of the Lord your God shall bring you into the land which your fathers possessed and you shall possess it, and He shall prosper you and multiply you more than your fathers.

H 30:6 And the Lord your God will circumcise your heart and the heart of your seed, to love the Lord your God with all your heart and with all your soul, that you may live.

PsJ And the Lord your God shall remove the foolishness of your heart and the foolishness of the heart of your children, for He shall abolish the evil impulse[69] from the world, and create a good impulse,[70] which shall counsel you to love the Lord your God with all your heart and with all your soul, so that your lives may be prolonged forever.

H 30:7 And the Lord your God will inflict all these curses upon your enemies and those who hate you, who have persecuted you.

PsJ And the Memra of the Lord your God shall send these curses upon the adversaries who oppressed you during your Dispersions, and upon the enemies who pursued and persecuted you.

H 30:8 And you shall return and listen to the voice of the Lord, and do all His commandments which I command you today.

PsJ   But you shall repent and obey the Memra of the Lord, and
           do all His commandments which I command you this day.

H   30:9 And the Lord your God will make you abundantly pros-
           perous in all the work of your hand, in the fruit of your
           body, and in the fruit of your cattle, and in the fruit of
           your land, beneficently; for the Lord will again rejoice over
           you beneficently, as He rejoiced over your fathers.

PsJ   And the Lord your God shall provide goodly abundance
           for you, so that you may prosper in all the work of your
           hands, in the children of your loins, and in the offspring of
           your cattle, and in the fruit of your land, beneficently; for
           the Memra of the Lord shall again rejoice over you and
           be good to you, just as He rejoiced over your fathers.

MI: וּמִשָּׁם יִקָּחֶךָ ... מִשָּׁם יְקַבֶּצְךָ . From the double expression
concerning the ingathering, PsJ infers that the event will be accomplished by Elijah and the Messiah.

In v. 6, the metaphorical expression, "and the Lord your God
shall circumcise your heart," PsJ interprets as the removal of
foolishness, the source of which is the tendency towards evil in
man, the evil impulse, which God Himself had created in man's
heart, but which later He regretted.[71] In Jewish eschatology, which
is here interwoven with the Messianic, the evil impulse, personified,
will be slain by God on the judgment day in the presence of both
the righteous and the wicked.[72] The reference to God's creating
a good impulse at the end of time does not exactly jibe with the
prevalent view that both the good impulse and the evil impulse
were placed in man from the beginning,[73] but this may be predi-
cated on the interpretation of Ezek. 36:26. The Targumist sees in
man's following of the good impulse, in directing his life to the
love of God, the road to eternal life. Repentance opens up this
avenue (v. 8), PsJ taking תָּשׁוּב , "you shall return," in the sense
of תשובה , "repentance." Prosperity and euphoria follow, v. 9.
In this Messianic framework, the enemies of Israel are treated
rather mildly, they are subject merely to curses, v. 7, while Israel
will repossess its own land, v. 5.

SUMMARY OF TARGUMIC INTERPRETATIONS
IN THE PENTATEUCH

Targum Onkelos is most sparing in its Messianic exegesis, and has Messianic references only to Gen. 49:10-12 and Num. 24:17-20, 23-24.

The Messiah is portrayed as a symbol of security, culture and refinement in Genesis, and in Numbers as a leader who will restore the political and military strength of Israel by gaining dominion over the entire world after he utterly destroys Rome. Jerusalem and its inhabitants will enjoy divine protection, represented by a rebuilt sanctuary. The social order will be undergirded by peace, prosperity, and righteousness, all under the influence of Torah which will become the universal law, and by the ideal of education, which will become a universal reality. Since O is composite, differing views are to be expected, here and there.

Targum Pseudo-Jonathan has Messianic references in its interpretations to Gen. 3:15; 35:21; 49:1, 10-12; Ex. 17:16; 40:9-11; Num. 23:21; 24:17-20, 23-24; Dt. 25:19; 30:4-9.

The Messianism in PsJ is not at all consistent. For example, in Num. 24:17 it is the Messiah who will vanquish Gog; in Ex. 40:11 this is to be achieved by the Ephraimite Messiah. In Dt. 30:4 the ingathering of the exiles is to be effected both by Elijah and by the Messiah. PsJ dips into the Messianic much more readily and freely than O, and he interprets as his fancy strikes him. Yet, considering the vast amount of Scriptural resources, he does not have an overabundance of Messianic references.

The picture of the Messiah as portrayed by PsJ embraces all the features found in O, and a number of others besides. The Messiah son of Ephraim is introduced, something which is not found in the Messianism of the official Targumim, whether to the Pentateuch or to the Prophets. The vindication of Israel and the destruction of its enemies will be accomplished by a blood-bath, performed by the Messiah, who as the aggressive war-lord of the future, will himself be covered with the blood of the slain foe. Notwithstanding this, the era which he inaugurates will mark the end of war, the establishment of peace, justice, and righteousness. The dispersed Jews will be gathered in, established once again on their own land, and will be purified by the elimination of the evil impulse and thereby will attain eternal life. This idea is tied with Torah and ethic, and hinges on the performance of the commandments. PsJ also discourages speculation as to the date of the advent of the Messiah.

The Fragmentary Targum contains Messianic interpretation in Gen. 3:15; 49:1, 10-12; Ex. 12:42; Num. 11:26; 24:7, 17-20, 23-24.

The Messianism of F is essentially the same as that both of O and PsJ, with several added features. F draws a comparison between Moses and the Messiah. He has the Messiah coming from Rome, not Palestine. He interprets the prophecy of Eldad and Medad as Messianic prophecy.

On the whole, the unofficial Targumim are more liberal with the Hebrew text in their Messianic exposition, than O and the LXX, V, and S versions. All the Targumim reflect rabbinic thought, generally, but sometimes they are completely independent of it and go beyond it. Their influence on Christian doctrine and V is discernible in Gen. 3:15, Num. 23:21 and 24:24.

CHAPTER II

THE MESSIANIC EXEGESIS OF THE
TARGUM TO THE PROPHETS

The only source used in this section is Targum Jonathan, abbreviated J, attributed to Jonathan b. Uzziel. It is the complete and official Targum to the Prophets, the only one that was considered authoritative and occupied a preeminent position as the Aramaic version of the Prophets. It is of one and the same mould as Targum Onkelos to the Pentateuch, and, like O, was used in the synagogue service. There is another Aramaic version of the Prophets, the Targum Yerushalmi, the Jerusalem Targum, which is fragmentary, and inconsequential, and is not even printed in the Rabbinic Bibles. It never did play a significant role in Jewish exegesis, but occasionally it is quoted by medieval Jewish commentators. The critical edition of Sperber served as the basic text, with comparative reference to Lagarde and the Warsaw edition of the Rabbinic Bible.

33

I SAMUEL

H 2:7 The Lord makes poor and makes rich, He brings low, He also lifts up.

J The Lord makes poor and makes rich, He brings low, He also exalts.

H 2:8 He raises up the poor out of the dust, He lifts up the needy from the dunghill, to make them sit with princes, and inherit a seat of honor; for the pillars of the earth are the Lord's, and He has set the world upon them.

J He raises up the poor from the dust; He lifts the needy from the dunghill, to make them sit with the righteous, the nobles of the world, giving them possession of the thrones of honor; for the deeds of the sons of men are revealed to the Lord. He prepares Gehenna below for the wicked, who transgress against His word,[1] but He establishes the world for the righteous, who will do His will.

H 2:9 He will guard the feet of His pious ones, but the wicked shall be silenced in darkness; for not by might shall a man prevail.

J The bodies of His servants, the righteous, He shall save from Gehenna, but the wicked shall be judged with Gehenna, with darkness, to make known that no one who relies on force shall be meritorious on the Day of Judgment.

H 2:10 Those who contend against the Lord shall be terrified; in heaven, He will thunder against them. The Lord shall judge the ends of the earth, and He shall give strength unto his king and exalt the horn of His anointed.

J The Lord shall shatter the adversaries who arise to do evil to His people; He shall blast them with a loud noise[2] issuing from Heaven. The Lord shall exact punishment from Gog[3] and from the marauding armies of the nations who come with him from the ends of the earth. He shall give strength to His king, and shall make great the kingdom of His Messiah.

MI: לְמַלְכּוֹ, "to His king," and מְשִׁיחוֹ, "His anointed," v. 10.

J is rather freely paraphrastic here. Occasionally we find a definite textual basis for his exegesis. Gehenna is adduced from בַּחֹשֶׁךְ, "in the darkness," v. 9. In v. 10, יַרְעֵם, "He will thunder" could have been taken in the meaning of תרועה, the blowing of the trumpet,[4] although J's language is ambiguous. "His adversaries" in v. 10, understood as Gog and his cohorts. "The poor" and "the needy" in v. 8 refer to the righteous.

In this passage the Messiah is a king, but mostly a symbol. The Messianic is interwoven with the battle of Gog, which God will wage, and with the idea of retribution.

LXX and *S* translate literally in v. 10.

V: ". . . and shall exalt the horn of his Christ."

I Sam.

H   2:35   And I will raise up for Me a faithful priest, who will do according to what is in My heart and in My soul; and I will build for him a secure house, and he shall walk before My anointed one all the days.

J   I will raise up before Me a trustworthy priest, who shall minister according to My word[5] and My will, and I will establish for him an enduring reign and he shall serve My Messiah[6] all the days.

It is uncertain whether this passage is Messianic, the Targumic text being vague. There is some slight possibility that it may be, judging from the context, and from the idea that an enduring reign will be established for the faithful priest.

II SAMUEL

The passage in II Sam. 7:11-16, which some interpreters regard as the basis of Messianism,[7] is not taken Messianically in the Targum.[8] As a matter of fact, J seems to go out of his way in v. 14 to soften the anthropomorphism which, according to Christian exegetes, makes the son of David the son of God, translating thus: "I shall be unto him as a father and he will be like a son[9] before Me." It would appear that J may be familiar with Christian exegesis on this passage, and, by implication, tries to counteract it, although some authorities are of the opinion that such a motive is not present in Targumic exegesis.[10]

II Sam.

H 22:28 And a humble people Thou dost save, but Thine eyes are on the haughty, Thou bringest them down.

J   The people of the house of Israel, who are called "a humble people" in his world, Thou art destined to redeem, and, by Thy Memra, Thou shalt bring low the mighty who lord over them.

H 22:29 Verily, Thou art my lamp, O Lord, and my Lord will illumine my darkness.

J   For Thou, O Lord, art He, the master, the light of Israel; and the Lord has brought me out of the darkness into the light, and has shown me the world which is destined to come for the righteous.

H 22:30 Verily, through Thee I can run down a troop, through my God I can scale a wall.

J   For by Thy Memra I will raise a mighty army, and by the Memra of my God I will conquer all the strongly fortified cities.

H 22:31 The God whose way is perfect, the word of the Lord has stood the test of time, He is the shield of all who take refuge in Him.

J   The way of God is perfect; the Torah of the Lord is choice; He is the strength of all who trust in Him.[11]

H 22:32 For who is God other than the Lord, and who is a rock other than our God?

J   Then, in consequence of the miracle and the deliverance which Thou shalt perform for Thy Messiah and for the remnant of Thy people who remain, all peoples, nations, and tongues shall confess, and say, "There is no God but the Lord;" verily, there is none besides Thee. And Thy people shall say, "There is none mighty, save our God."

There is no specific MI in the Hebrew text. The general tone of the context probably suggested the Messianic, and v. 32 is seized upon to reflect the historical situation in which the Moslems are the dominant political power, and their theological core is very similar to the Jewish. This does not mean that the Targumist conceives the Messiah as already come; it merely means that he sees in the political and theological framework of the Moslems a pattern which might be acceptable in the Messianic age. This passage provides evidence to place the *terminus ad quem* of Targum Jonathan subsequent to the rise of Islam.[12]

In v. 28, "humble people" is identified as Israel, because of its low political estate. The contrast of light and darkness in v. 29 suggests the reward of the righteous in the World-to-Come. In v. 30 גְּדוּד , is interpreted as "a mighty army;" אֲדַלֶּג־שׁוּר , "jumping over a wall," suggests conquering the walled, fortified cities. In v. 32, note the contrast between what the nations say and what Israel responds. Israel has not changed its monotheistic views nor adopted the Moslem faith.

There are no RP to this Targumic interpretation.

S: Verse 32, "For there is no God excepting the Lord, and there is none mighty, save God."

A: "For there is no God but the Lord." [13]

II Sam.

H   23:1   And these are the last words of David, the oracle of David, son of Jesse, the oracle of the man who was raised up by the Most High, the anointed of the God of Jacob, the sweet singer of the Psalms of Israel.

J   These are the pronouncements of prophecy of David, which he prophesied concerning the end of the world, concerning the days of consolation which are destined to come. Said David, the son of Jesse, said the man who was anointed to the Messianic kingship by the Memra of the God of Jacob, who was fit to be appointed because of the sweetness[14] of his Psalms of Israel.

H   23:2   The spirit of the Lord spoke through me, and His word was on my tongue.

J   Said David: "I speak these things by the spirit of divine prophecy, His holy words I formulate in my mouth."

H   23:3   Said the God of Israel, the Rock of Israel speaking to me: "Ruler of men shall be the righteous, ruling in the fear of God,"

J   Said David: "The God of Israel spoke to me, the Mighty One of Israel, who has dominion over the sons of men, the One who judges in truth, and He decided[15] to appoint for me a king, he is the Messiah, who is destined to arise and rule in the fear of the Lord.

H   23:4   And as the light of the morning, when the sun shines on a cloudless morning; as grass sprouts from the earth by sunshine and rain."

J   Fortunate are you righteous ones. You have performed righteous deeds, by virtue of which your[16] glory shall be as radiant as the light of the morning which grows increasingly stronger, and like the sun, which is destined in the future to have three hundred and forty three times the effulgence it had during the seven days.[17] In addition to that, you shall be exalted, and it shall be well with you, who have longed for the coming years of consolation, lo, as the farmer during the years of drought longs for the coming down of rain on the ground."

H 23:5 Verily, should not my house be so with God? Verily, an everlasting covenant He has made with me, ordered in all things, and secured. Verily, all my salvation and all my desire, verily, will He not make them sprout?

J Said David, moreover: "My house is in the presence of God, for He has made an eternal covenant with me that my kingdom shall be as firmly established as the immutable laws of nature,[18] vouchsafed even unto the World-to-Come; and since all my desires and wishes are fulfilled by Him, no other kingdom shall endure in His presence."

MI: הָאַחֲרֹנִים, which J understands as "the latter things," in v. 1, and the second מוֹשֵׁל, "ruler," v. 3, which he takes as referring to the Messiah. In v. 1, מָשִׁיחַ, "anointed" refers to David, not to the Messiah, and is descriptive of the Messianic assignment to the Davidic line.

J resorts to paraphrase and exegetical complement. He supplies what he thinks is missing from the text. He takes key words and builds them into his own Messianic-eschatological interpretations, such as the morning light, and the radiance of the sun, which he expounds in terms of reward for the righteous. The quantitive effulgence of the eschatological sun is based on Is. 30:26, the calculation being 7 x 7 x 7, for a total of 343.[19] Rabbinic thought on this theme varied somewhat. There was one opinion that the sun was originally much more powerful than it came to be, and that this pristine radiance would be restored in the Messianic age.[20]

V: Verse 1, ". . . concerning the Christ of the God of Jacob." The rendering *"de Christo"* is based on the reading עַל, instead of the Masoretic עָל, which J follows.

S: "Said the man who set up the furrow of the Messiah."

I KINGS

H 5:13a[21]   And he spoke of the trees, from the cedar which is in the Lebanon to the hyssop which comes out of the wall.

J   And he prophesied concerning the kings of the house of David who were destined to rule in this world and in the world of the Messiah.[22]

MI: הָאֶרֶז , "the cedar," on the basis of Ezek. 17:22 and הָאֵזוֹב , "the hyssop" used for purification in preparation for holiness.

That Solomon should attest to the coming of the Messiah is borne out by Ps. 72, which the Targum interprets Messianically.[23]

ISAIAH

H   4:1   And seven women shall take hold of one man on that day, saying, "We will eat our own bread and wear our own clothes, only let your name be called upon us: take away our shame."

J   At that time, seven women shall seize one man, saying, "We will eat of our own, and of our own we will clothe ourselves, only let your name be applied to us. Remove our disgrace."

H   4:2   On that day the branch of the Lord shall be beautiful and glorious, and the fruit of the land shall be the pride and splendor of the survivors of Israel.

J   At that time, the Messiah of the Lord shall be a joy and an honor, and those who fulfill the Torah[24] shall be great and glorious to the remnant of Israel.

H   4:3   And he who is left in Zion and he who remains in Jerusalem, "holy" shall be said of him, whoever is inscribed for life in Jerusalem.

J   He who remains shall return to Zion, and he who fulfills the Torah shall be established in Jerusalem. Everyone who is inscribed for eternal life shall be called "holy"; he shall see the consolation of Jerusalem.

H   4:4   When the Lord has washed away the filth of the daughters of Zion and cleansed the blood from her midst, by a spirit of judgment and by a spirit of burning.

J   When the Lord removes the filth of the daughters of Zion, and makes the shedding of innocent blood in Jerusalem disappear from its midst, by the word of justice, the final[25] word.

H   4:5   And the Lord will create over every building of Mt. Zion and over her assemblies a cloud by day and smoke, and a shining, flaming fire by night; for over all the glory shall be a canopy.

J   Then the Lord shall create over the entire sanctuary of Mt.

Zion and over the place which houses His Shekinah, a dark cloud of glory shading it during the day as a dark cloud; and as a flaming fire at night; for in addition to the glory which was promised to it, the Shekinah shall protect it like a canopy.

H   4:6   And a booth shall provide shade from heat by day, and a refuge and a shelter from the torrent and the rain.

J   And over Jerusalem there shall be My cover of clouds[26] to shade it from the heat during the day, and as a secret hiding place to provide shelter from the storm and from the rain.

MI: Verse 2, צֶמַח , "branch," a favorite term of Messianic connotation, here used with the name of the Lord.

"The fruit of the land" is interpreted as those who live the life of Torah, associated with the thought that the study of Torah is the greatest of those performances, the fruit of which a man eats in this world.[27] In v. 5, עַל is understood as "in addition to," "besides."

The term "branch" frequently leads to a Messianic deduction.[28] Here it is the branch of the Lord, usually scion of David. The Messianism emphasizes righteousness and justice, and divine protection for the holy city.

Is.

H   9:5²⁹   For to us a child has been born, a son has been given to us; and the government shall be upon his shoulder. The wonderful counsellor, the Mighty God, the Eternal Father, has called his name "Prince of Peace."

J   The prophet announced to the house of David that: "A boy has been born unto us, a son has been given untó us, who has taken the Torah upon himself to guard it;³⁰ and his name has been called by³¹ the One who gives wonderful counsel, the Mighty God, He who lives forever: 'Messiah,' in whose day peace shall abound for us.

H   9:6   Of the increase of his government and of peace, there will be no end, upon the throne of David, and over his kingdom, to establish it and to sustain it with justice and righteousness, from now and forever. The zeal of the Lord of Hosts shall do this.

J   He shall make great the dignity of those who labor in the Torah and of those who maintain peace, without end; on the throne of David and over his kingdom, to establish it and to build it in justice and in righteousness,³² from this time forth and forever. This shall be accomplished by the Memra of the Lord of Hosts."

There is no specific MI in the Hebrew, except perhaps indirectly from "throne of David" and "his kingdom" in v. 6. The context is Messianic, and J supplies the name "Messiah," which is not stated in the text. His rendering of יֻלַּד and נִתַּן , both in the perfect tense in Hebrew, and וַתְּהִי and וַיִּקְרָא, the imperfect with *waw* conversive, by the Aramaic perfect which puts the action in the past, leads us to suspect that the Targumist may have had Hezekiah in mind as the Messiah, reflecting a trend of thought which had adherents during the Targumic period.³³ Hezekiah's acceptance of the Torah and his raising the dignity of those who live by it, are ideas also found in rabbinic lore. The Talmud depicts Hezekiah as a zealous defender and champion of the Torah.³⁴ Such an interpretation would in no way constitute a contradiction or change of emphasis in J's Messianic thinking. Since it is assumed that J is the work of many Targumists stretching over centuries, if this is the present interpretation of Is. 9:5, it merely reflects the thinking of one individual or perhaps several, but does not change the mainstream of J's Messianism. But there is no sure way of ascertaining what was in the Targumist's mind. Those who do not accept the view that Hezekiah was the Messiah point to the final (closed) *mem* (‎ם) in the middle of the word ‎לְסַרְבֵּה, the Masoretic *ketib* in v. 6, as proof of their contention that though God may have thought to make Hezekiah the Messiah, He eventually changed His mind.[35]

The ideas in this passage point to the Messiah as a symbol of very high educational level of society, expressed in Torah, which is to be the guide to conduct, and justice and righteousness in the affairs of state. The active agent of redemption is here depicted as the Memra.

All versions take this passage as Messianic, at least on the strength of its implications.

Is.

H 10:24 Therefore, thus says the Lord, God of Hosts: "Do not be afraid of Assyria, O My people dwelling in Zion, though he strike you with the rod and lift up his staff against you, in the manner of Egypt.

J Therefore, thus says the Lord, God of Hosts: "O My people who dwell in Zion, do not fear the Assyrian when he smites you with his rule and throws his tyranny at you, as in the manner of Egypt.

H 10:25 For in a little while, very soon, My anger will come to an end, and My wrath will be towards their destruction."

J For in a very little while, the curses shall come to an end for you of the house of Jacob, and My anger shall be against the nations who practice abomination, to destroy them."

H 10:26 Then the Lord of Hosts will stir up a scourge against him, like the smiting of Midian at the rock of Oreb; and His rod will be over the sea, and He will lift it, in the manner of Egypt.

J And the Lord of Hosts shall bring[36] upon him a scourge as the smiting of Midian at the cleft of Oreb, and his tyranny[37] shall be removed from you, as the tyranny of Pharaoh was removed at the sea, and mighty deeds shall be performed for you, as in Egypt.

H 10:27 And it shall come to pass on that day, that his burden shall be removed from off your shoulder, and his yoke from off your neck, the yoke shall be destroyed by the oil.

J It shall come to pass at that time, that his tyranny shall be removed from you, and his yoke from upon your neck, and the nations shall be shattered before the Messiah.

MI: שֶׁמֶן , "oil," taken in the sense of anointing.

This passage is significant because it draws a parallel between the deliverance from Egypt and the deliverance which is to be effected by the Messiah, the re-enactment of the original drama of liberation. It is also of interest because the Messianic scene is laid in an Àssyrian historical setting, leading again to the suspicion that the Targumist may have had Hezekiah in mind. In any event, this is an illustration of the genius of Targumic exegesis, which takes a text such as this, "and the yoke shall be destroyed by the oil," and gives it meaning and purpose, albeit of his own making. Note that RSV does not know what to do with this phrase and omits it completely from the body of the translation, following LXX.

RP: " 'Thy name is as ointment poured forth' (Song of Songs 1:3): Thy name is magnified by everyone who busies himself with the oil of the Torah. This is the opinion of R. Judan, who explained: 'And the yoke shall be destroyed because of oil' (Is. 10:27), the yoke of Sennacherib would be destroyed because of Hezekiah and his followers who occupied themselves with the oil of the Torah." (Song of Songs Rabbah to 1:3 (2).

	Is.	
H	11:1	And there shall come forth a shoot from the stump of Jesse, and a branch shall grow out of his roots.
J		And a king shall come forth from the sons of Jesse, and the Messiah shall be anointed from among his children's children.
H	11:2	And there shall rest upon him the spirit of the Lord, the spirit of wisdom and understanding, the spirit of counsel and might, the spirit of knowledge and fear of the Lord.
J		And upon him shall rest the spirit of divine prophecy,[38] the spirit of wisdom and sagacity, the spirit of counsel and might, the spirit of knowledge and fear of the Lord.
H	11:3	And He shall make him sensitive by the fear of the Lord, so that he shall not judge by the sight of his eyes, nor shall he reprove by the hearing of his ears;
J		And the Lord shall bring him near to the worship of Him.[39] He shall not judge according to the sight of his eyes, nor shall he reprove according to the hearing of his ears.[40]
H	11:4	But he shall judge the poor in justice and shall reprove with equity for the humble of the land; and he shall smite the earth with the rod of his mouth, and with the breath of his lips he shall slay the wicked.
J		But he shall judge the poor in truth, and shall reprove in faithfulness for the needy of the people.[41] He shall smite the guilty of the land with the word of his mouth, and with the speech of his lips he shall slay Armilus[42] the wicked.
H	11:5	And justice shall be the girdle of his waist and faithfulness shall be the girdle of his loins.
J		The righteous shall surround him, and the faithful shall be near him.
H	11:6	The wolf shall dwell with the lamb and the leopard shall lie down with the kid, and the calf and the young lion and the fatling together, and a small child leading them.

J   In the days of Israel's Messiah, peace shall abound in the land; the wolf shall dwell with the lamb, and the leopard shall lie down with the kid, and the calf and the lion and the fatling together, and a small suckling child leading them.

H   11:7   And the cow and the bear shall feed together, their young shall lie down; and the lion, like the ox, shall eat straw.

J   And the cow and the bear shall graze, their young ones shall lie down together, and the lion shall eat straw like the ox.

H   11:8   And the suckling child shall play over the hole of the asp, and over the viper's den the weaned child put his hand.

J   The suckling child shall play laughingly over the hole of the winding serpent, and the weaned child shall put his hands over the eyeballs of the venomous snake.

H   11:9   They shall not hurt or destroy in all My holy mountain, for the earth shall be filled with the knowledge of the Lord as the waters cover the sea.

J   They shall do no harm nor destroy on all My holy mountain, for the land shall become full of the knowledge of the worship of the Lord, as the waters cover the sea.

H   11:10   And on that day the root of Jesse shall stand as an ensign of the peoples; him shall the nations seek and his resting-place shall be glorious.

J   And it shall be at that time that kings shall obey the descendant[43] of Jesse, who is destined to stand as a sign to the nations, and the place of his dwelling shall be glorious.

H   11:11   And it shall be on that day that the Lord will for a second time extend His hand to recover the remnant which is left of His people, from Assyria and from Egypt and from Pathros and from Cush and from Elam, and from Shinar and from Hamath and from the islands of the sea.

J   At that time the Lord shall again show His might a second time, to deliver the remnant of His people who are left, from Assyria, from Egypt, from Pathros, from India, from Elam, from Babylon, from Hamath, and from the islands of the sea.

H 11:12 And He will raise an ensign to the nations and He will gather the dispersed ones of Israel, and the scattered ones of Judah He will gather in from the four corners of the earth.

J And He shall raise a sign to the nations, and shall gather together the scattered of Israel, and shall bring back the Dispersion of Judah from the four directions of the earth.

H 11:13 Then the jealousy of Ephraim shall depart, and those of Judah who harass shall be cut off; Ephraim shall not be jealous of Judah and Judah shall not harass Ephraim.

J The jealousy of the tribe[44] of Ephraim shall vanish, and they who oppress the tribe[44] of Judah shall be destroyed. They of the tribe[44] of Ephraim shall not be jealous of the tribe[44] of Judah, and they of the tribe of Judah shall not oppress the tribe of Ephraim,

H 11:14 And they shall swoop down upon the shoulder of the Philistines to the west, together they shall plunder the peoples of the east; Edom and Moab shall be within the grasp of their hands, and the Ammonites shall obey them.

J But they shall put their shoulders together to smite the Philistines who are in the west; together they shall despoil the people of the east; they shall put forth their hand against Edom and Moab, and the Ammonites shall become subservient to them.

H 11:15 And the Lord will destroy the tongue of the sea of Egypt and will wave his hand over the river with his scorching wind, and will smite it into seven rivulets and let men go across dry-shod.

J And the Lord shall dry up the tongue of the sea of Egypt, and He shall raise the striking power of His might over the Euphrates by the word of His prophets, and He shall smite it into seven brooks which they can cross dryshod.[45]

H   11:16   And there shall be a highway for the remnant who are left
            of His people, from Assyria, as there was for Israel on the
            day he came up from the land of Egypt.

J   And there shall be a paved road for the remnant of His
            people who are left from the Assyrian, just as there was
            for Israel on the day of their going up from the land of
            Egypt.

MI: חֹטֶר מִגֵּזַע יִשָׁי , "a shoot from the stump of Jesse," and
וְנֵצֶר מִשָּׁרָשָׁיו , "and a branch of his roots" in v. 1, and שֹׁרֶשׁ יִשַׁי ,
"the root of Jesse," in v. 10.

"The spirit of the Lord" in v. 2 is the spirit of prophecy. In
v. 4, "the wicked" is Armilus, for Romulus, for Rome, who takes
the place of Gog in late rabbinic legend,[46] who will be obliterated
by the Messiah's word. The term צֶדֶק in v. 5 is understood as
צדיקים "the righteous ones," instead of the abstract; similarly,
וְהָאֱמוּנָה , as "the faithful ones," instead of "faith." "Girdle" is
taken as metaphor in a double sense, "round about," and "very
near." In v. 8, מְאוּרַת ,"den," is interpreted as that which permits
אוֹר , "light," to enter, i.e., the eyeball. In v. 14 בְּכָתֵף , "with
shoulder," is taken in the nominative rather than the accusative.
In vv. 11 and 14, the anthropomorphism "the hand" of God is
rendered by "His power." In v. 15 we find a genuine VR, וְהֶחֱרִיב ,
"and He shall dry up" instead of the Masoretic וְהֶחֱרִים , "and He
shall destroy." Also in v. 15, the *hapax legomenon* בַּעְיָם , is interpreted as the "strength of word," and coupled with רוּחוֹ , "His
spirit," is rendered, "by the word of His prophets."

The following features are discernible in this Messianic picture: The Messiah, of the Davidic line, will be gifted with
prophecy, wisdom, understanding and faith in God. As judge, he
will penetrate to the true core beneath the surface, will dispense
judgment with equity, but will be merciful in his dealings with
those who have been the victims of social injustice. Injustice he
will correct by word of mouth, which will serve as his weapon
against the final foe of Israel. The righteous and the faithful shall

come into their own. Peace will be established, even to the extent of a change in the nature of the savage beast, including the beastly nature in man, by a recognition of the divine. The Messiah will rule over the nations from his glorious capital, the sanctuary. There will be an ingathering by God of the Hebrew exiles, both of the Northern Kingdom and of Judah, who will now be reconciled and join forces to destroy their historic enemies. The Euphrates, the scene of exile and dispersion will be struck dry, just as was the sea in the story of the Exodus, enabling the remnant of Israel to be delivered in a re-enactment of the Exodus. The dominant motif throughout is peace and harmony in nature, within and without the individual, on the local level and in the world as a whole.

No one had seen the grim horror of war any more clearly than had Isaiah. No one could project an ideal future in terms opposite of carnage more beautifully than he. No one had been more intimately involved in the divine deliverance of Judah from the hand of the Assyrian than was this prophet, and no one had more insight than he into the merit of the Davidic, which he construed as the factor of grace which enabled Judah to survive, and which made it imperative that Ephraim should return to the Davidic fold. Here was the architect of Messianism. All this the Targumist senses, and he conveys it powerfully, yet delicately, and with extreme sensitivity, in his rendering of the prophetic text. The Targumic interpretations of Isaiah tend to bear out an assumption of ours, that the psychodynamic origins of Messianism are to be found in the Assyrian crisis.

Conspicuously absent is any specific reference to Torah. The general idea of Torah is, of course, implied in prophecy, spirit, wisdom, justice and righteousness, all of which are prominent here. But it is barely possible that this Targumic exposition adheres to the thought expressed by R. Hanin, who said: "Israel will have no need of the teaching of the King Messiah in the future, for it says: 'Him shall the nations seek' (Is. 11:10), but Israel shall not," [47] and teaching, naturally, means Torah.

RP: Is. 11:1 is generally accepted in rabbinic lore as a reference to the Messiah. It is used in the Midrash as a point of discussion in a story to the effect that the Messiah was born when the Temple was destroyed, and it will be rebuilt again close upon his coming.[48] This is adduced from the fact that Is. 11:1 follows immediately upon 10:34, which speaks of the Lebanon falling, a metaphor interpreted as the fall of the Temple.

The other versions, following the text closely, all resound with the Messianic tone, but none is as explicit as the Targum.

Is.

H 14:29 Rejoice not, Philistia, all of you, that the rod that smote you is broken, for from the root of the serpent shall go forth a viper and its offspring will be a flying serpent.

J Rejoice not, all you Philistines, that the dominion which had held you in servitude is shattered, for the Messiah shall come forth from the descendants of Jesse, and his deeds among you shall be like those of the flying serpent.[49]

H 14:30 And the first-born of the poor shall feed, and the needy shall lie down in safety; but I will kill your root by starvation, and what is left of you he shall slay.

J The poor of the people shall be provided with food, and, in his day, the humble shall dwell securely; but your sons[50] will die by famine, and the rest of your people he shall slay.

MI: מִשֹּׁרֶשׁ, "from the root," in v. 29, presumably the root of Jesse.

The Messianic here, as in most of Isaiah, seems to be a reference to Hezekiah. The rejoicing of the Philistines was occasioned by the death of Uzziah, who had smitten the Philistines severly, as is borne out by II Chron. 26:6 ff. Is. 14:28 could indicate that the rejoicing continued until the death of the weakling Ahaz. The prophet promises more trouble for Philistia under a descendant of her enemy, Hezekiah.[51]

Is.

H   16:1   They have sent lambs to the ruler of the land from Sela in the desert to the mountain of the daughter of Zion.

J   They shall send tribute[52] to the mighty Messiah of Israel, because they were like a desert to the mountain of the congregation of Zion.[53]

H   16:2   Like the bird that flutters over a nest that has been emptied, so shall be the daughters of Moab at the fords of the Arnon.

J   And he[54] shall be like a bird whose nestlings are removed; the daughters of Moab shall be carried off and exiled[55] to Arnon.

H   16:3   Bring counsel, do justice, make your shade at high noon like the night; hide the driven ones, do not expose the fugitive.

J   Take counsel, get advice! Make your shade during midday like the night.[56] Hide the homeless and do not expose the ones who are scattered.

H   16:4   Let my driven ones dwell with you, O Moab, hide them from the destroyer. When the oppressor is no more, and destruction has ceased, and he who tramples under foot has disappeared from the land.

J   O Kingdom of Moab, let the exiles settle among you; shelter them from the despoilers. For the oppressor has come to an end, the despoiler has been destroyed, all who used to trample to death have vanished from the earth.[57]

H   16:5   Then a throne shall be established in loving kindness, and on it shall sit in faithfulness in the tent of David, one who judges and seeks justice, and is swift to do righteousness.

J   Then the Messiah of Israel shall establish his throne in goodness, and shall occupy it in truth, in the city of David, judging, demanding justice and doing righteousness.

MI: מוֹשֵׁל אָרֶץ , "ruler of the land," v. 1, which he takes universally as the ruler of the earth, rather than merely of the land, and כָּסֵא , "throne," v. 5.

In v. 1 מִדְבָּרָה, "desert," is understood as being the attitude of Moab towards Israel. Verse 4b, according to the Targumist, refers to Moab. In v. 5, the "tent of David" is rendered the "city of David."

The Messianism is mild, with no vindictiveness, implying only universal rule, justice and righteousness.

RP: The Midrash understands v. 5 Messianically.[58] Significantly enough, all of the major rabbinic commentators take it as a reference to Hezekiah.[59]

V: Verse 1, *"Emitte agnum, Domine, dominatore terrae, de petra,"* etc. The Lamb is the ruler of the earth. There is a Christological twist here, Messianism probably based on the Targum.

Gray[60] suggests the possibility that v. 5 is a later interpolation of a Messianic passage.

Is.

H   28:5   On that day the Lord of Hosts shall be for a crown of glory
            and for a diadem of beauty for the remnant of His people;

J   At that time the Messiah of the Lord of Hosts shall be a
            wreath of joy and a crown of praise to the remnant of His
            people,

H   28:6   And for a spirit of justice to him who sits in judgment, and
            for strength to those who turn back the battle at the gate.

J   And a proclamation of true justice to those who preside in
            court, that they may render right decisions; and to accord
            victory to those who go forth to battle, and return them to
            their homes in peace.

This passage is one of those rarities, with no MI in the Hebrew
text, and which is, on the whole, inexplicable. The Hebrew simply
reads   יְהֹוָה צְבָאוֹת , "the Lord of Hosts." It is unlikely that the
Targumist considered God to be the Messiah, in the light of our
knowledge of Targumic Messianism. Furthermore, Messiah and
Lord of Hosts are not in apposition, the expression being משיחא
דיוי צבאות   which is literally as translated above. And there
is no RP.

DEUTERO-ISAIAH

Is.

H 42:1 Behold My servant, I uphold him, My chosen one whom My soul desires. I have placed My spirit upon him, he will bring forth justice to the nations.

J Behold, My servant, the Messiah,[61] whom I bring near, My chosen one, in whom My Memra takes delight; I will place My holy spirit upon him, and he shall reveal My law to the nations.

H 42:2 He will not cry out, nor raise his voice, nor make his voice heard out in the open.

J He shall not cry, nor shout, nor raise his voice on the outside.

H 42:3 A bruised reed he will not break, and a flickering wick he will not extinguish; in truth he will bring forth justice.

J The humble, who are like the bruised reed, he shall not break, and the poor of My people, who are like candles, he shall not extinguish; he shall truly bring forth justice.

H 42:4 He will not falter nor will he be crushed until he sets justice in the earth; and the islands shall wait for his teaching.

J He shall not faint and he shall not tire until he establishes justice in the earth; and the isles shall wait for his Torah.

H 42:5 Thus says God, the Lord, the Creator of the heavens, He who extended them; who spreads out the earth and what comes out of it; who gives life to the people who are upon it, and spirit to those who walk on it.

J Thus says the God of the universe, the Lord, who created the heavens and suspended them, who established the earth and its inhabitants, who gives life to the people who are upon it and spirit to those who walk in it.

H 42:6 "I am the Lord, I have called you in righteousness, and I have taken you by the hand; and I have formed you and

I have given you as a covenant of the people, as a light of the nations.

J   "I, the Lord, have anointed you in righteousness, and have firmly taken you by the hand, and established you, and I have given you as a covenant of the people, as a light of the nations.

H   42:7   To open blind eyes, to bring out the prisoner from the prison, from the dungeon those who sit in darkness.

J   To open the eyes of the house of Israel, who have been blind to the Torah; to bring back their Dispersions from among the nations, they, who are like prisoners; and to deliver them, who are imprisoned like prisoners in darkness, from the servitude of the empires.

H   42:8   I am the Lord, that is My name, and My glory to any other I shall not give, nor My praise to graven images.

J   I am the Lord, that is My name, and My glory, which I have revealed unto you, I will not give to any other people, nor My praise to those who worship idols.

H   42:9   The former things, behold, they have come to pass, and new things I now declare; before they blossom I announce them to you."

J   The former things, behold, they have come to pass, and new things I declare; even before they occur I announce them to you."

MI: עַבְדִּי, "My servant," and בְּחִירִי , "My chosen one," in v. 1. Employing the method of exegetical complement, J supplies what he thinks is missing in the text, namely, the Messiah.

In v. 2, there is a genuine VR, יִשָּׁאג , "he will roar" for the Masoretic יִשָּׂא , "raise." In v. 3, the exegetical complement is again employed to explain the bruised reed and the flickering wick. In v. 5, the unusual expression הָאֵל is interpreted as *the* God, par excellence, the universal God. וְצֶאֱצָאֶיהָ , "what comes forth from the earth" is understood as "inhabitants," for men are God's primary concern. In v. 6, "I have called you," means "I have anointed you"; this is the call, and refers to the Messiah. Verses 6 and 7 detail the Messianic purpose. In verse 7, the blind eyes are those of Israel, who have been blind to the heritage of Torah which is theirs.

The Messianic picture is lofty, spiritual; the Messiah, though a liberator, is gentle. His primary concern is with Israel, but he will also benefit mankind, by giving them laws or instruction. The dispensing of justice and righteousness sets the Messianic tone.

There are no RP which interpret this passage Messianically.

LXX: "Jacob is My servant . . . Israel is My chosen one," [62] which, of course is not Messianic, and which was the prevalent rabbinic interpretation of this passage,[63] as well as its counterpart in Is. 52:13 ff.

V: Messianic by implication and explanatory note. Matt. 12:18 also utilizes Is. 42:1 as a Messianic prooftext, referring to Jesus.

S: Literal, with Messianic overtones.

Is. 42:19 is a problem to the exegete who interprets the servant Messianically, inasmuch as it characterizes the servant as blind. Note how the Targum renders this passage: "Is it not so, that if the wicked repent they shall be called 'My servants,' and the guilty to whom I have sent my prophets (also)? But the wicked are destined to be punished for their deeds; however, if they repent they shall be called 'servants of the Lord.'" In this interpretation, "blind" refers to the wicked, who do not see what is right.

The servant in Is. 44:26 is likewise not rendered Messianically: "He fulfills the words of His servants, the righteous," etc.

Is.

H 43:10   "You are My witnesses," says the Lord, "and My servant whom I have chosen, that you may know and believe Me, and that you may understand that I am He; before Me there was fashioned no God, and after Me there shall be none."

J   "You are witnesses before Me," says the Lord, "and My servant is[64] the Messiah, whom I have chosen; that you may know and believe Me, and that you may understand that I am He[65] who was from the beginning, and also that all eternities belong to Me, and besides Me there is no God."

MI: וְעַבְדִּי , "And My servant."

The implication of this passage is that the coming of the Messiah is a testimonial to the existence of God, even as Israel itself is a witness to Him. It is to be a vindication of Israel and Israel's faith.

Is.

H 52:13 Behold, My servant shall prosper, he shall be exalted, lifted up, and very high.

J Behold, My servant the Messiah shall prosper; he shall be exalted and great and very powerful.

H 52:14 As many were astonished at you, so his appearance was marred from that of man, and his resemblance from that of sons of man,

J As the house of Israel, their appearance darkened among the nations, and their bright countenance darkened among the children of men, looked for him many days.

H 52:15 So shall he startle many nations. Kings shall shut their mouth because of him; for that which was not told to them they shall see, and that which they have not heard they shall understand.

J So shall he scatter many nations. Kings shall be silent concerning him, they shall place their hands on their mouths, for that which had not been related to them they have seen, and that which they had not heard they will understand.

H 53:1 Who will believe what we have heard, and the arm of the Lord to whom has it been revealed?

J Who would have believed this, our good tidings, and the powerful arm of the might of the Lord, for whom is it now revealed?

H 53:2 And he came up before him like a sapling, and like a root out of the dry ground; he had no beauty and no majesty, that we should look at him, and no appearance that we should delight in him.

J The Righteous One[66] shall grow up before Him, lo, like sprouting plants; and like a tree that sends its roots by the water-courses, so shall the exploits[67] of the holy one[68] multiply in the land which was desperate for him. His appearance shall not be a profane[69] appearance, nor shall the awe of him be the awe of an ignorant person, but his countenance shall radiate with holiness, so that all who see him shall become wise through him.[70]

H   53:3   He was despised and forsaken of men, a man of torments and acquainted with infirmity, and like one from whom one hides his face, he was despised and we esteemed him not.

J   Then he shall be contemptuous of, and bring to an end, the glory of all the kingdoms; they shall become weak and afflicted, lo, like a man in pain and accustomed to illness, and like us, when the Shekinah had departed from us, leaving us despised and without esteem.

H   53:4   Surely he has borne our infirmities and carried our torments, but we considered him smitten with disease, stricken by God, and afflicted.

J   Then he shall seek pardon for our sins, and our iniquities shall be forgiven for his sake; though we are considered stricken, smitten by God, and afflicted.

H   53:5   And he was wounded by our transgressions, he was crushed by our iniquities; the chastisement of our peace was upon him, and with his stripes we were healed.

J   And he shall rebuild the Temple, which was profaned because of our sins, and which was surrendered because of our iniquities; through his instruction, his peace shall abound for us, and when we teach[71] his words our sins shall be forgiven us.

H   53:6   All of us like sheep have wandered, we have turned each in his own direction, but the Lord has inflicted upon him the iniquity of us all.

J   All of us were scattered like sheep, we were exiled, each in his own direction, but it is the will of God to pardon the sins of all of us on his account.

H   53:7   He was oppressed and humbled himself, but he did not open his mouth, like a sheep that is led to the slaughter, and like a ewe that is silent before those who shear it, he opened not his mouth.

J   He asked in prayer and was answered, and it was accepted
           even before he could open his mouth; he shall deliver the
           mighty of the nations like a lamb to the slaughter; and like
           a lamb that is silent before its shearers, there shall be none
           to open his mouth and say a word against him.

H   53:8 By oppression and by judgment was he taken; and as for
           his generation, who gave it any consideration? For he was
           cut off from the land of the living, stricken because of the
           transgression of My people.

J   He shall gather in our exiles from their pain and punish-
           ment. Who shall be able to recount the wonders which
           shall be performed for us in his days, for he shall remove
           the domination of the nations from the land of Israel. And
           the sins which My people have committed, he shall account
           unto them.[72]

H   53:9 And he assigned his grave with the wicked, and with a rich
           man in his death, though he had done no violence and
           there was no deceit in his mouth.

J   And he shall deliver the wicked into Gehenna, and those
           rich in possessions which we had lost, taken by force at
           death; so that those who commit sin shall not prevail and
           shall not speak deceitful things with their mouth.[73]

H   53:10 But the Lord desired to crush him by disease, if his soul
           would offer itself in restitution, so that he might see his
           seed prolong his days, and that the purpose of the Lord
           shall prosper in his hand.

J   It is the will of the Lord to purify and to acquit as innocent
           the remnant[74] of His people, to cleanse their souls of sin,
           so that they may see the kingdom of their Messiah, have
           many sons and daughters, enjoy long life, and observe the
           Torah of the Lord, prospering according to His will.

H   53:11 From the travail of his soul, he shall see and be satisfied
           by his knowledge; My servant shall account the righteous
           as righteous to the multitudes, and he shall bear their
           iniquities.

J   He shall save them from the servitude[75] of the nations, they
             shall see the punishment of their enemies and be sated with
             the spoil[76] of their kings. By his wisdom he shall vindicate
             the meritorious, in order to bring many to be subservient[77]
     ?   to the Torah, and he shall seek forgiveness for their sins.

H   53:12   Therefore, I will give him a portion among the great, and
             he shall divide the spoil with the mighty; because he poured
             out his life to the death and was numbered with trans-
             gressors; yet he bore the sin of many, and for transgressors
             he will intercede.

J   Then I will apportion unto him the spoil of great nations,
             and he shall divide as spoil the wealth of mighty cities, be-
             cause he was ready to suffer martyrdom that the rebellious
             he might subjugate to the Torah. And he shall seek pardon
             for the sins of many and for his sake the rebellious shall
             be forgiven.

MI: עַבְדִּי , "My servant," in 52:13.

There is one VR in this passage: עֲלָיו , "at him," for the
Masoretic עָלֶיךָ , "at you," in 52:14.

This is an excellent example of Targumic paraphrase at its best.
It is not translation, nor is it loose and meaningless commentary,
but a reworking of the text to yield what the Targumist desires it
to give forth. He snatches at words and phrases in the Hebrew,
usually the key word or phrase in the verse, and on the basis
of these he structures his interpretation. The mechanics of derivation in this instance, in detail, may easily be detected by comparing
the Targumic version with the text.

The striking feature of the Targumic Messianism here is a reworking of Deutero-Isaiah's conception of the Suffering Servant
into an exalted, proud, and aggressive personality, a champion
who takes up the cudgels for the despised and downtrodden and
suffering Israel, who wields destructive power over their enemies
and subjugates mighty kings in their behalf. He also restores
Israel to national dignity, rebuilds its sanctuary, is a champion

of Torah, metes out judgment to the wicked, and consigns them
to Gehenna. A new Messianic note is sounded in the intercessory
power of the Messiah, who pleads for pardon for Israel's sins,
which are forgiven for his sake. While this is intercession, it is
not vicarious atonement; for the Messiah, though he is the servant
and is willing to submit to martyrdom, does not suffer.

Churgin[78] is of the opinion that this Targumic passage stems
from the time when Bar Kokhba stood at the head of warring
armies, and therefore the Targumist could not have taken literally
the picture in Is. 52-53, but rather makes a glorious presentation
of the Messiah, who is for him present in the flesh at that time.
Churgin asserts that Is. 53:5 points clearly to Bar Kokhba. This
may well be, as other Targumic passages point in the same direction.[79] At the very least, this passage shows beyond a doubt that
in Jewish Messianic thought of the Targum there is no room
whatsoever for a suffering and dying Messiah. If there were such,
the Targumist would have to look no farther for Biblical support
than the Suffering Servant passages, yet from what he does with
them, it is obvious what his thoughts are.

RP: " 'Behold My servant shall prosper' (Is. 52:13), this is
the King Messiah . . . 'he shall be exalted,' above Abraham . . .
'and lifted,' above Moses . . . 'and very high,' above the ministering
angels." [80]

LXX: Literal but not Messianic, in line with 42:1.

V: Messianic overtones and undertones in translation.

S: Literal, but with Messianic implication.

It is of unusual significance that early Christianity, which had
appropriated LXX as its primary Scriptural source, could find
no Messianic comfort in LXX's version of the Servant passages,
and had to fall back on that Targumic-rabbinic viewpoint which
understood the passages Messianically. Also significant is the
demonstration that the early Church, in this instance at least, did
not tamper with the text of LXX to support its Christological
claims.

JEREMIAH

H   23:1   "Woe to the shepherds who destroy and scatter the flock of My pasture," says the Lord.

J   "Woe unto the leaders who destroy and scatter the people over whom My name is called," says the Lord.

H   23:2   Therefore, thus says the Lord, the God of Israel about the shepherds who tend my people: "You have scattered My flock and have driven them away, and you have not attended to them. Behold I will visit upon you your evil deeds," says the Lord.

J   Therefore, thus says the Lord, the God of Israel, concerning the leaders who lead my people: "You have scattered My people, and made them exiles, and have not been concerned about them. Behold, I will visit upon you the evil of your deeds," says the Lord.

H   23:3   "And I, Myself, shall gather the remnant of My sheep from all the lands where I have driven them, and I will bring them back to their fold, and they shall be fruitful and multiply.

J   "And I will gather the remnant of My people from all the countries to which I had exiled them, and I will return them to their place, and they shall increase and become numerous.

H   23:4   And I will raise up over them shepherds and they shall fear no more nor be dismayed, nor shall any be missing," says the Lord.

J   And I will raise up for them leaders and they shall provide for them, and they shall fear no more, nor be broken,[81] nor moved," says the Lord.

H   23:5   "Behold, days are coming," says the Lord, "and I will raise up for David a righteous branch and he shall reign as king, and be wise, and do justice and righteousness in the land.

J   "Behold, days are coming," says the Lord, "when I will raise up for David a righteous Messiah, and he shall reign as king, and prosper, and shall enact a righteous and meritorious law in the land.

H 23:6 In his days Judah will be saved and Israel will dwell securely. And this is the name which He shall call him, 'The Lord is our righteousness.'

J In his days they of the house of Judah shall be delivered, and Israel shall live in security. And this is the name which they shall call him: 'May vindication be accomplished for us by the Lord in his day.' [82]

H 23:7 Therefore, behold days are coming," says the Lord, "when they shall no longer say, 'As the Lord lives, who brought up the children of Israel from the land of Egypt,'

J Therefore, behold, days are coming," says the Lord, "when they shall no longer be talking about the might of the Lord who brought the children of Israel up out of the land of Egypt,

H 23:8 But rather, 'As the Lord lives, who has brought up and brought back the seed of the house of Israel from the northern land and from all the lands where I have driven them,' and they shall dwell on their own soil."

J But they shall be talking about the might of the Lord who brought up and led the descendants of the house of Israel from the north country and from all the countries to which I had exiled them, and they shall dwell on their own land."

MI: צֶמַח , "branch" in v. 5.

J explains the metaphor of the shepherds explicitly, as meaning leaders, whom he holds responsible for Israel's troubles, as does the Hebrew text. In vv. 7 and 8 he eliminates the language of the oath in God's name, which he finds objectionable, and simply renders the passage as referring to people recounting the miracle of deliverance, the future one to supplant the historic recounting of the wonder of the Exodus from Egypt. Cf. Berakot 12b.

The Messiah is the righteous king who will provide favorable dispensation and practice righteousness, and be the symbol of peace and security. The actual ingathering of the exiles will be performed by God.

RP: "What is the name of the King Messiah? R. Abba b. Kahana said: His name is 'the Lord';[83] as it is stated, And this is the name whereby he shall be called, The Lord is our righteousness (Jer. 23:6)." Lamentations Rabbah 1:51.

"R. Samuel b. Nahmani quoted R. Jonathan as saying: 'Three are designated by the name of the Holy One blessed be He, namely, the righteous, the Messiah, and Jerusalem . . . the Messiah, as it is stated, And this is the name," etc. (Jer. 23:6). Baba Bathra 75b.

LXX, V, and *S* all carry Messianic implications. Verses 7 and 8 are missing in LXX.

Jer.

H 30:8 "And it shall come to pass on that day," says the Lord of Hosts, "I will break his yokc from off your neck, and I will burst your bonds, and strangers shall no longer enslave him.

J "And it shall come to pass at that time," says the Lord of Hosts, "that I will break the yoke of the nations[84] from off your necks, and I will loosen your chains, and the nations shall no longer make slaves of Israel.

H 30:9 But they shall serve the Lord their God and David their king, whom I will raise up for them.

J But they shall worship the Lord their God and obey the Messiah, the son of David, their king, whom I will raise up for them.

H 30:10 And you, do not fear, O My servant Jacob," says the Lord, "and do not be dismayed, O Israel; for behold, I will save you from afar, and your seed from the land of their captivity. And Jacob shall return, and have quiet and ease, and none shall make him afraid.

J And you, fear not, O My servant Jacob," says the Lord, "nor be dismayed, O Israel! For behold, I deliver you from afar, and your children from the land of their[85] Dispersions, and they of the house of Jacob shall return and be at ease and live in security, and there shall be none to frighten them.

H 30:11 For I am with you," says the Lord, "to save you. Verily, I will make an end of all the nations where I have scattered you, but of you I will not make an end. And I will chasten you justly, but I will not make a clean sweep of you."

J For My Memra comes to your aid to deliver you," says the Lord. "Verily, I will make a complete end of all the nations among whom I have scattered you, but I will not make a complete end of you. I will bring sufferings upon you to correct you, but with clemency, for I will not completely destroy you."

MI: דָּוִד מַלְכָּם , "David their king," v. 9 which J interprets not

literally, but to refer to the Messianic Davidic offshoot, rather than
to David himself.

In v. 8 the Targumist, through the exegetical complement, explains in full that "his yoke" means the yoke of the nations, and
likewise that this is what is meant by "strangers." In v. 11, the
apparent anthropomorphism of God being with Israel, in the
physical sense, is softened by the use of the Memra. The Biblical
לְמִשְׁפָּט, is interpreted as "with clemency," the righteousness, or
mercy, of God. J takes וְנַקֵּה as "to make a clean sweep of," "to
exterminate."

The significant Messianic feature is the explanation of the
Hebrew text in v. 9, which is either a poetic figure or the prophet's
actual wishful thoughts of a David redivivus, so that for the
Targum it becomes the Messiah, son of David.

RP: "R. Judah quoted Rav as saying: 'In the future, the Holy
One, blessed be He, will raise up for Israel another David, as it
is stated, And David their king, whom I will raise up for them
(Jer. 30:9). It is not written whom I have raised up for them,
but whom I will raise up for them' " [86] Sanhedrin 98b.

LXX: This entire section and more (vv. 6-27) is missing.

V: Messianic, in tone and by explanatory note.

S: Literal, Messianic in tone.

Jer.

H 30:21 "His prince shall be one of his own, and his ruler shall come out of the midst of him, and I will bring him near and he shall approach Me, for who is this who would venture by himself to approach Me?" says the Lord.

J "Their king shall be anointed from them, and their Messiah shall be revealed from among themselves. I will draw them near and dedicate them[87] to My worship, for who is this one whose heart desires to be drawn to My worship?" says the Lord.

MI: וּמֹשְׁלוֹ , "and his ruler," in keeping with the eschatological nature of the Hebrew context.

The third singular accusative suffix of וְהִקְרַבְתִּיו , "and I will bring him near," as well as וְנִגַּשׁ "and he shall approach," is referred back to Israel, rather than to the king, and hence J renders these in the plural.

Here the Messiah stands as the symbol of the religious regeneration of Israel, and of their rapprochement with God.

Jer.

H 33:12 Thus says the Lord of Hosts: "There shall once again be, in this place, which is waste, without man or beast, and in all of its cities, a habitation of shepherds making their flocks to lie down.

J   Thus says the Lord of Hosts: "There shall again be, in this place which is waste, without man or even beast, and in all its cities, dwellings, houses for the shepherds to rest, and sheepfolds for the sheep.

H 33:13 In the cities of the hill country, in the cities of the Shephelah, and in cities of the Negev, and in the land of Benjamin, and in the surroundings of Jerusalem, and in the cities of Judah, the flocks shall once more pass by, by the hands of one who counts them," says the Lord.

J   In the cities of the hill country, in the cities of the Shephelah, and in the cities of the south, in the land of the tribe of Benjamin, in the surroundings of Jerusalem, and in the cities of the tribe of Judah, the people shall yet rehearse the words of the Messiah," says the Lord.

H 33:14 "Behold, days are coming," says the Lord, "when I will fulfill the good word which I have spoken to the house of Israel and about the house of Judah.

J   "Behold, days are coming," says the Lord, "when I will fulfill the firm word which I have spoken concerning the house of Israel and the house of Judah.

H 33:15 In those days and at that time I will cause to sprout for David a righteous branch who will do justice and righteousness in the land.

J   In those days and at that time, I will raise up for David a righteous Messiah, who shall enact a righteous and meritorious law in the land.

H 33:16 In those days Judah shall be saved and Jerusalem shall reside securely; and this is what he will call her: 'The Lord is our righteousness.' "

J   In those days, they of the house of Judah shall be delivered, and Jerusalem shall dwell in security and this is the name which they shall call her: 'May vindication be accomplished for us by the Lord in her midst.' " [88]

H   33:17 For thus says the Lord: "There shall never be cut off from David a man sitting on the throne of the house of Israel.

J   For thus says the Lord: "There shall never cease for David a man sitting on the throne of the kingdom of the house of Israel.

H   33:18 And as for the priests, the Levites, a man shall not be cut off in My presence, offering up burnt offering and burning the grain offering and preparing the sacrifices, all the days."

J   And for the priests, the Levites, there shall never cease a man before Me to offer up burnt offerings, to offer the sacrifice, and to perform the sacrificial functions [89] all the days."

H   33:19 And the word of the Lord came to Jeremiah, saying:

J   And word of divine prophecy came to Jeremiah, saying:

H   33:20 "Thus says the Lord: If you can annul My covenant with the day and My covenant with the night, so that day and night will not be in their proper time,

J   "Thus says the Lord: Just as it is impossible for the covenant which I have made with the day and with the night to be nullified, so that day and night will not occur at their appointed time,

H   33:21 Then also My covenant can be annulled with David, My servant, so that he will not have a son reigning on his throne, and with the Levites, the priests, My ministers.

J   So also cannot the covenant which I have established with David My servant be broken, so that he will not have a son reigning on his throne, and the Levitical priests who minister before Me.

H 33:22   As the host of heaven cannot be counted, and the sands of the sea cannot be measured, so will I multiply the seed of David, My servant, and the Levites who minister unto Me."

J   As it is impossible for the host of heaven to be counted and for the sands of the sea to be measured, so will I make numerous the descendants of David My servant, and the Levites who minister before Me."

H 33:23   Now the word of the Lord came to Jeremiah saying:

J   And the word of prophecy was from the Lord with Jeremiah saying:

H 33:24   "Have you not observed what these people have said: 'The two families which the Lord has chosen, and He has now rejected.' Thus they despise My people, so that they are no longer a nation in their presence.

J   "Have you not seen what this people are speaking, saying: 'The two families which the Lord has chosen, He has rejected them.' And they have scandalized My people, so that they can no more be a people to minister before Me as had been assigned to them.

H 33:25   Thus says the Lord: If it were not for My covenant with the day and the night then I could not have set a fixed order in heaven and earth;

J   Thus says the Lord: Just as it is impossible to nullify the covenant which I have established with the day and the night, as I have not appointed the fixed laws of heaven and earth to disappear;

H 33:26   And I would also reject the seed of Jacob and David My servant, and would not take of his seed to be rulers over the seed of Abraham, Isaac and Jacob. Verily, I will change their fortunes and I will have mercy upon them."

J   Similarly, I will not cast off the descendants of Jacob and David My servant, from whose sons there shall come those who rule over the descendants of Abraham, Isaac and

Jacob, for I will bring back their Dispersions and I will have mercy upon them."

MI: מוֹנֶה , "the one who counts," in v. 13, and צֶמַח in v. 15, "branch."

In v. 20 and 21, J elaborates on the meaning of the Hebrew, and couches the thought in language which seems to be more explicit to him, and which he believes can be more readily comprehended.

From the Messianic standpoint, the passage adds nothing new, but does point up, as does the Hebrew, the unbreakable, eternal covenant between God and David which must result in the advent of the Messiah.

LXX: Literal.

V: Messianic implications.

S: Messianic overtones.

EZEKIEL

H 17:22 Thus says the Lord God: "And I Myself will take a twig
from the top of the lofty cedar, and I will put it forth; and
I will break off from the topmost of its young branches, a
tender one, and I Myself will plant it on a high and lofty
mountain.

J   Thus says the Lord God: "I Myself will bring near a
child[90] from the dynasty[91] of the house of David, which
is likened to the tall cedar, and I will raise him up from
his children's children; I will anoint and establish him by
My Memra like[92] a high[93] and exalted mountain.

H 17:23 On the high mountain of Israel I will plant it, and it shall
put out branches and bear fruit, and it shall become a noble
cedar; and they shall dwell under it all birds; every fowl
shall dwell in the shade of its branches.

J   On the mountain of the Holy One of Israel will I establish
him, and he shall gather together armies and build forts
and become a mighty king; and all the righteous shall rely
upon him, and all the humble shall dwell in the shade of
his kingdom.

H 17:24 And all the trees of the field shall know that I the Lord
have brought low the lofty tree, I have raised aloft the
low tree; I have dried up the green tree, and have made the
dry tree to blossom. I the Lord have spoken, and I will
do it."

J   All the kings of the nations shall know that I, the Lord,[94]
have humbled the kingdom which was mighty, and have
made mighty the kingdom which was weak: I have humbled the kingdom of the nations which was mighty as a
green tree, and have made mighty the kingdom of the house
of Israel which was as weak as a dried out tree. I, the
Lord, have decreed by My Memra, and I will fulfill it."

   MI: מִצַּמֶּרֶת הָאָרֶז , "of the top of the cedar," and מֵרֹאשׁ יְנִקוֹתָיו ,
"of the top of its branches," v. 22.
   In v. 23, J follows the Masoretic text in taking מָרוֹם , "lofty,"

to be in construct state with יִשְׂרָאֵל , "Israel," and understands
the phrase as "God." The Targumist explains the allegory of the
trees. The cedar is the house of David, which God is going to reestablish. The dried-out tree which God will strengthen is Israel.
Note that there is no explicit use of J's usual term for the Messiah
משיחא . The restoration of David occurs in the Biblical text of
Ezekiel as a future hope. Everything points to a Targumic Messianic innuendo, but the Messiah's designation as such is absent.

Ezek.

H 34:20   Therefore, thus says the Lord God to them: "Behold, I
           Myself will judge between the fat sheep and the lean sheep.

J   Therefore, thus says the Lord God to them: "Behold, I
           reveal Myself, and I will judge between the rich man and
           the poor man.

H 34:21   Because you thrust with side and shoulder, and push all
           the weak with your horns, till you have scattered them
           abroad,

J   Because you have oppressed with wickedness and bru-
           tality,[95] and with your brute strength have broken the
           weak, until you have scattered them among the countries,[96]

H 34:22   I will save My flock and they shall no more be despoiled;
           and I will judge between sheep and sheep.

J   I will deliver My people, and they shall no longer be handed
           over as spoil; and I will judge between man and man.

H 34:23   And I will set up one shepherd over them, and he shall
           feed them, My servant David; he shall feed them, and he
           shall be their shepherd.

J   I will set up over them one leader who shall provide for
           them, My servant David; he shall provide for[97] them and
           he shall be their leader.[97]

H 34:24   And I the Lord will be their God, and My servant David
           prince among them; I the Lord have spoken.

J   And I, the Lord, will be their God, and My servant David
           shall be king[98] in their midst. I, the Lord, have decreed
           this by My Memra.

H 34:25   And I will make them a covenant of peace, and will cause
           evil beasts to cease out of the land; and they shall dwell
           securely in the wilderness, and sleep in the woods.

J   I will cut[99] a covenant of peace for them, and remove the
           wild beast from the land, so that they may live securely
           in the wilderness and grow old in the forests.

H 34:26 And I will make them and the places round about My hill a blessing; and I will cause the rain to come down in its season; they shall be rains of blessing.

J I will settle them all around My Temple, and they shall be blessed; I will send down for them the early rain in its season; they shall be rains of blessing.

H 34:27 And the tree of the field shall yield its fruit, and the earth shall yield her produce, and they shall be secure in their land; and they shall know that I am the Lord, when I break the bars of their yoke, and deliver them out of the hand of those who enslaved them.

J And the tree of the field shall yield its fruit, and the earth shall yield its harvest, and they shall be secure on their land; and they shall know that I am the Lord when I break their mighty yoke and save them from the hand of those who are enslaving them.

H 34:28 And they shall no more be spoil to the nations, nor shall the beast of the earth devour them; but they shall dwell securely, and none shall make them afraid.

J They shall no longer be the spoil of the nations, and the kingdoms of the earth shall not destroy them, but they shall dwell in security, with no one to frighten them.

H 34:29 And I will raise up for them a plant of renown, and they shall be no more consumed by hunger in the land, and they shall not bear the shame of the nations any more.

J And I will raise up for them an enduring[100] plant, and they shall never again be exiles of famine in the land, and they shall never again be humiliated[101] by the nations.

H 34:30 And they shall know that I the Lord their God am with them, and that they, the house of Israel, are My people, says the Lord God.

J And they shall know that I am the Lord their God, My Memra is their help, and that they are My people, the house of Israel, says the Lord God.

H 34:31   And you My sheep, the sheep of My pasture, are men, and
            I am your God, says the Lord God."

J   And you, My people, the people over whom My name is
            called, you are the house of Israel, and I am your God, says
            the Lord God."

MI: רֹעֶה , "shepherd," in v. 23.

The references to David in vv. 23 and 24 are rendered literally, and the term "Messiah" does not occur, although the poetic picture of shepherd and flock are interpreted to mean leader and people, and the prophecy is decidedly a future hope. In v. 25 the reference in the Hebrew to wild beast is also rendered literally, in spite of the fact that the normal Targumic exegesis would find in this a good opportunity to interpret it as the yoke of the foreigner. Were it not for this fact, the enduring plant in v. 29 might be taken Messianically, but with the Targum to Ezekiel it is a problem.

Ezek.

H 37:21 And say unto them: Thus says the Lord God: "Behold, I will take the children of Israel from among the nations, where they have gone, and I will gather them from every side, and bring them to their own land.

J Prophesy unto them: Thus says the Lord God: "Behold, I bring in the children of Israel from among the nations to which they were exiled, and I will gather them from all around and bring them into their own land.

H 37:22 And I will make them one nation in the land, upon the mountains of Israel and one king shall be for all of them.

J And I will make them one nation in the land on the holy mountain of Israel, and one king shall serve them all as king; they shall no longer be two nations, nor shall they be divided into two kingdoms any more.

H 37:23 And they shall defile themselves no more with their idols, nor with their detestable things, nor with any of their transgressions; but I will save them out of all their dwelling-places in which they have sinned, and will cleanse them; and they shall be My people and I will be their God.

J They shall no more defile themselves with their idols, and with their detestable things, and with all their rebellions, but I will save them out of all their dwellings in which they sinned,[102] and will purify them; and they shall be My people, and I will be their God.

H 37:24 And My servant David shall be king over them and one shepherd there shall be for all of them; they shall walk in My ordinances, and observe My statutes, and do them.

J And My servant David shall be king over them; and they shall all have one leader; and they shall walk in My laws and shall keep my statutes and observe them.

H 37:25 And they shall dwell in the land that I gave unto Jacob My servant, in which your fathers dwelt; and they shall dwell therein, they, and their children, and their children's children, forever; and David My servant shall be their prince forever.

J   And they shall dwell in the land which I gave to My servant, to Jacob, in which your fathers lived; and they and
their children and their children's children shall dwell therein forever, and David My servant shall be their king forever.

H   37:26   And I will make a covenant of peace for them—it shall
be an everlasting covenant with them; and I will be gen-
erous with them, and multiply them, and I will set My
sanctuary in the midst of them forever.

J   I will make a covenant of peace for them, it shall be an
everlasting covenant with them, and I will bless them and
make them numerous, and place My sanctuary in their
midst forever.

H   37:27   And My dwelling-place shall be over them; and I will be
their God and they shall be My people.

J   I will make My Shekinah rest in their midst; I will be their
God and they shall be My people.

H   37:28   And the nations shall know that I am the Lord who sancti-
fies Israel, when My sanctuary shall be in the midst of them
forever."

J   And the nations shall know that I, the Lord, sanctify Israel, when My sanctuary is in the midst of them forever."

MI: וְרוֹעֶה , "shepherd," in v. 24.

With the exception of several interpretive renderings, this is
virtually a verbatim literal translation of the Hebrew. The exceptions are: רוֹעֶה , "shepherd," in v. 24, rendered "leader"; נָשִׂיא ,
"prince," in v. 25, rendered "king"; וּנְתַתִּים , "and I will give
them," in v. 26, which J takes as an ellipsis, rendered "and I will
bless them"; and מִשְׁכָּנִי , "My dwelling," in v. 27, which is interpreted as שכינה , "Shekinah."

The picture here is one of a regenerated, purified Israel, once
more living in a convenantal relationship with God, indicated by a
rebuilt Temple, restoration to its own land and national sover-
eignity, with the Northern Kingdom and Judah re-united under
David, which may either be a resurrected David, or merely a
symbolic representation of the Davidic line.

From the standpoint of Messianic exegesis, the Targum to Ezekiel presents a major problem. Not once is the Messiah designated as such, even where the Hebrew text presents ample opportunity for Messianic interpretation and designation. The preceding passages are a clear case in point. There is another passage which makes the case even stronger. Ezek. 21:31-32 (vv. 26 and 27 in the English versions), which lends itself to Messianic interpretation,[103] is rendered by the Targumist historically, thus:

Ezek.

H   21:31   Thus says the Lord God: "Remove the mitre and take off the crown. This isn't the same. Exalt what is low, and bring down what is high.

J   Thus says the Lord God: I will remove the mitre from Seraiah, the High Priest,[104] and take off the crown of King Zedekiah. Say that both the one and the other will not endure in his place, but they shall surely be exiled. It[105] shall be given to Gedaliah the son of Ahikam, to whom it did belong.

H   21:32   A ruin, ruin, ruin will I make of it. Such as this there never has been, until he comes to whom righteousness belongs, and to him I will give it.

J   The sins which they have sinned, as their very own sins,[106] they shall be punished for. Likewise for this one[107] it shall not be established for them, for I will bring upon him the punishment of Ishmael the son of Nethaniah,[108] and will deliver him into his hand.

This passage is made by the Targumist to fit into the historical picture of the final days of the Kingdom of Judah, down to the detailed mention of the names of the historical persons who took part in that drama. The reference which might have been Messianic, עַד בֹּא אֲשֶׁר לוֹ הַמִּשְׁפָּט , "until he comes, to whom justice belongs," is applied by the Targumist to Ishmael the son of Nethaniah, the murderer of Gedaliah.

Why the Targum to Ezekiel avoids any specific Messianic designation must remain a matter of speculation. This problem has never been pointed out before, not even by such a profound observer as Churgin.

It cannot be argued that the Targum to Ezekiel came under greater censorial pressure than the Targum to the other books of the Bible, and hence had to suppress any explicit mention of the Messiah.[109] It is generally conceded that the official Targumim originated in Palestine and were redacted in Babylon.[110] There were historical interludes in Palestine under Roman rule when the expression of such Jewish ideas carried the death penalty with it,[111] and Messianic thought in particular was regarded as treasonable. But this did not restrain Jewish sages[112] either from thinking or teaching, and some of them were martyred on that account. Their views and interpretations survived the temporary edicts of suppression, and, for that matter, Rome itself. So we cannot draw the line and make an exception of this Targum, the more so since it predicts the destruction of Rome by rendering Ezek. 39:16 thus: "There, too, shall be thrown the slain of Rome, the city of noisy crowds." [113]

Nor can it be maintained that the Targum to Ezekiel is more literal and less paraphrastic than the rest of J to the Prophets. We have seen how explicit it is on Ezek. 21:31-32, elaborating on the text to the full. Even if it were more literal, this in itself would not sustain the point, since there is no more literal Aramaic version than Targum Onkelos to the Pentateuch, and yet O gives an outright Messianic interpretation to Gen. 49:10 and Num. 24:17. By the same token, if the Targum to Ezekiel expected the Messiah to take the form of a return of David in person, as some of the rabbis did,[114] he still could have specified that this would be the Messiah, which he scrupulously avoids. Furthermore, Ezekiel should lend itself more readily to Messianic exegesis by virtue of its Gog passages, which had become intimately associated with the advent of the Messiah in rabbinic thought, and yet even these the Targum renders without Messianic reference.

One possible conclusion presents itself, and that is that the Targumist or Targumists originally responsible for the Targum to

Ezekiel did not find Messianism as imperative an issue as some of the others, and hence did not look for it in the text nor give expression to it in the translation. Whether this points to Babylonian rather than Palestinian origin, thus breaking down the generally accepted theory of Palestinian authorship of all the Targumim, or merely to a period of national tranquillity and the absence of foreign pressure, cannot be determined for certain. It does, however, indicate an eschatological, non-Messianic outlook, similar to the one expressed by R. Hillel: "Israel will have no Messiah, since they have already consumed him (his coming was consummated) in the days of Hezekiah." [115] It seems probable not only that this Targum is of different authorship from that of the rest of J,[116] but what is even more significant, it follows a different current of thought. Perhaps most remarkable of all is the fact that this relatively non-Messianic version went through so many hands in the course of centuries without alteration of these passages, or the eventual inclusion of more definitely Messianic glosses.

RP: "And so it shall be in the future world, And David My servant shall be their prince forever." (Ezek. 37:25). Genesis Rabbah (NV) 97, Soncino p. 987.

LXX: All the Ezekiel passages cited here are rendered literally, but with Messianic overtones.

V: All of these passages are taken Messianically.

S: Messianic implications.

HOSEA

H 2:2[117]   And the children of Judah and the children of Israel shall
be gathered together, and they shall designate for themselves one head, and they shall go up from the land, for
great shall be the day of Jezreel.

J   And the children of Judah and the children of Israel shall
be gathered together as one, and they shall appoint for
themselves one head, of the house of David, and they shall
go up from the land of their Dispersion, for great shall be
the day of their ingathering.

MI: ראשׁ , "head."

Utilizing the exegetical complement, and understanding the text
as elliptical, J explains "head" as the Davidic line, and "the land"
as the land of their Dispersion, both lacking in the Hebrew. Here,
as in the Targum to Ezekiel, the Messiah is not designated as such,
but this passage is included here in view of 3:3 ff. Jezreel is taken
as the ingathering of the exiles, perhaps in the belief that then
Israel would truly be firmly planted by God, which is one meaning
of the word.

Hos.

H   3:3   And I said unto her: "You shall sit solitary for me many days; you shall not play the harlot, and you shall not be any man's wife; nor will I be yours."

J   Prophet, say unto her: "O congregation of Israel, your sins caused you to be exiled many days. Attend to My worship, do not go astray, and do not worship idols, then I, too, will in the future have compassion upon you."

H   3:4   For the children of Israel shall dwell many days without king, and without prince, and without sacrifice, and without pillar, and without ephod or teraphim.

J   For the children of Israel shall dwell many days without a king from the house of David, and without one exercising dominion over Israel, and without anyone offering acceptable sacrifice in Jerusalem, and without pillar in Samaria, and without ephod and idolatrous oracles.

H   3:5   Afterward shall the children of Israel return, and seek the Lord their God, and David their king; and shall come trembling unto the Lord and to His goodness in the end of days.

J   After that the children of Israel shall repent and seek the worship of the Lord their God, and they shall obey the Messiah, the son of David, their king, and he shall direct[118] them to the worship of the Lord; and great shall be His goodness which shall come to them at the end of days.

MI: דְּוִיד מַלְכָּם , "David their king," in v. 5, explained as the Messiah.

In v. 3, for the homiletical purpose of framing the discourse between God and wayward Israel, J reads the imperative וֶאֱמֹר , "and say," instead of the Masoretic וָאֹמַר , "and I said." The language for admonition to the woman not to stray is interpreted as admonition to Israel not to depart from God. מֶלֶךְ , "king," in v. 4 means Davidic king. The sacrifice is the legitimate offering at Jerusalem. The pillar, ephod, and oracle represent the idolatrous practices of the Northern Kingdom. The King David of the Text is interpreted as the Messiah at the end of time.

Hos.

H 14:5[119] I will heal their backsliding, I will love them freely; for My anger is turned away from him.

J I will accept them in repentance, will forgive their sins and love them, when they willingly repent, for My anger has turned from them.

H 14:6 I will be as the dew unto Israel; he shall blossom as the lily, and cast forth his root as Lebanon.

J My Memra shall be like the dew unto Israel; they shall blossom like the lily, and dwell on their mighty land like the cedar[120] of Lebanon which sends forth its roots.[121]

H 14:7 His branches shall spread, and his beauty shall be as the olive tree, and his fragrance as Lebanon.

J They shall have many sons and daughters, and their countenance shall be as the radiance of the candelabrum of the sanctuary, and they shall be as fragrant as spicy incense.

H 14:8 They shall return, they that dwell under his shadow; they shall grow corn, and shall blossom as the vine; the fragrance thereof shall be as the wine of Lebanon.

J They shall be gathered in from their Dispersion, shall live in the shade of their Messiah, and the dead shall live, and goodness shall abound in the land. The record [122] of their goodness shall continue without interruption, like the memory of the trumpet sounds accompanying the ritual libation of wine[123] in the Temple.

MI: בְּצִלּוֹ , "in his shade," v. 8, with the Messianic implied in third masculine singular suffix.

In v. 5 מְשׁוּבָתָם "their backsliding," is taken as תְּשׁוּבָתָם , "their repentance." "Shoots" in v. 7 refers to abundance of offspring, "the olive" is interpreted as the olive oil used in the candelabrum in the Temple, and "fragrance" as that of the Temple incense. In v. 8, יְחַיּוּ , "they shall grow grain," is read יִחְיוּ , "they shall live," and refers to the resurrection of the dead; "corn" is taken as prosperity, and "wine" as the Temple libation. "Dwell in his shade," indicates protection, security.

The Messianic description is one of moral regeneration of Israel, its forgiveness by God, the ingathering of exiles, security, abundance and quality of children, a state of goodness, and the eschatological element of the resurrection of the dead, which is a rarity for the Messianism of official Targumim, though there is a liberal sprinkling of it in their non-Messianic eschatological exegesis.

The prevalent rabbinic interpretation of בְּצִלּוֹ , "in his shade," v. 8, applies it to God in His protection of proselytes.[124]

V: Verse 8, refers to converts, the prevalent rabbinic view, but it also carries strong Messianic meaning.

MICAH

H   4:8   And you, Migdal-eder, the hill of the daughter of Zion, unto you it shall come; the former dominion shall come, the kingdom of the daughter of Jerusalem.

J   And you, O Messiah of Israel, who have been hidden away from the sins of the congregation of Zion, the kingdom is destined to come to you, and the former dominion shall be restored to the kingdom of the congregation of Jerusalem.

MI: מִגְדַּל עֵדֶר , "tower of the flock," the tower, strength, being the Messiah, and the flock, Israel.[125]

בַּת , "daughter," is understood as congregation, both with Zion and with Jerusalem.

The idea that the Messiah will be hidden away, possibly from the time of Creation, untouched by the sins of Israel, is a reflection of apocalyptic rabbinic thinking, as well as Christian.[126] The pristine splendor of the kingdom, is probably a reference to the rule of David. The preceding verses are eschatological, and, to the Targumist, this Messianic passage falls right in line.

There are no RP for the Messianic interpretation of this verse.

V: Messianic, probably under the influence of the Targum.

Mic.

H 5:1[127] And you, O Bethlehem Ephrathah, who are little to be among the families of Judah, out of you shall one come forth for Me who is to be ruler in Israel; whose goings forth are from of old, from ancient days.

J And you, O Bethlehem Ephrath, you who were too small to be numbered among the thousands of the house of Judah, from you shall come forth before Me the Messiah, to exercise dominion over Israel, he whose name was mentioned from before, from the days of creation.[128]

H 5:2 Therefore will He give them up, until the time that she who is in travail has brought forth; then the rest of his brethren shall return with the children of Israel.

J Then they shall be handed over for[129] the length of time it takes a woman in labor to give birth, and the children of Israel shall rely upon the rest of their brethren.[130]

H 5:3 And he shall stand, and shall feed his flock in the strength of the Lord, in the majesty of the name of the Lord his God; and they shall abide, for then shall he be great unto the ends of the earth.

J And he shall arise and rule with the might of the Lord,[131] in the exalted name of the Lord his God; and they shall be gathered in from the midst of their Dispersions, for now his name shall be great unto the ends of the earth.

MI: מוֹשֵׁל , "ruler," in v. 1.

The latter part of v. 1 in the Hebrew text would tend to support the doctrine of a pre-existent Messiah, which is not found in rabbinic thought.[132] The rabbinic conception, that the name of the Messiah was premundane,[133] is voiced by the Targumist. Verse 2 is the source of the notion of the pangs of the Messiah, the world in travail before the advent,[134] as well as the proof-text for the contention of Rav, that the Messiah will not come until nine months after the wicked kingdom, i.e. Rome, had spread its hegemony over Israel, and the rest of the world.[135]

All the ancient versions sense the Messianic implications of these verses in Micah, though as usual, LXX less so than the others.

HABAKKUK

Habakkuk 3:13 is interpreted by the Targumist as allegory reflecting the early history of Israel, among the other historical events in God's deliverance of Israel, and the Hebrew מְשִׁיחֶךָ , "Thy anointed," is merely rendered by its Aramaic equivalent, with possible reference to David. It is not Messianic. Neither is it taken Messianically by LXX. V, however, takes it as definitely referring to Christ.

Hab.

H   3.17   For though the fig tree shall not blossom, neither shall fruit be in the vines; the labour of the olive shall fail, and the fields shall yield no food; the flock shall be cut off from the fold, and there shall be no herd in the stalls,

J   For the kingdom of Babylon shall not endure, nor will it exercise dominion over Israel. The kings of Media shall be slain, and the mighty ones of Greece[136] shall not succeed. The Romans shall be destroyed, and shall not levy the tax[137] from Jerusalem.

H   3:18   Yet I will rejoice in the Lord, I will exult in the God of my salvation.

J   Then, in consequence of the miracle and deliverance which Thou shalt perform for Thy Messiah and for the remnant of Thy people who remain[138] they shall give thanks thus, says the prophet: "I take joy in the Memra of the Lord, I rejoice in God, who accomplishes my deliverance."

MI: There is no specific MI in the text, but the Targumist apparently adduces the Messianic meaning from the context.

In v. 17, the pastoral language is interpreted as referring to the historical, the four world powers, who dominated the Jews. Though the imperfect tense is used in each case, the reference to the tax levied against Jerusalem by the Romans indicates that this was written during Roman hegemony, when the matter of paying tribute was a burning issue with the Jewish people. It has even been suggested that this passage reflects the contemporary scene when the Procurator Quirinius instituted the census, which aroused the people to rebellion, 6-7 C.E.[139] If this be so, then v. 18 may express the hope that the Messiah, the leader of this rebellion, would succeed in throwing off the yoke of Rome. The leader of this rebellion was Judas the Galilean, a zealot who had the backing of the school of Shammai.[140] His very name, יהודה, "Judah," might have been Messianically attractive. All this, of course, is speculation, but speculation with some measure of plausibility. Whether or not the Targumist had Judas the Galilean in mind, he certainly is expecting the Messiah, and imminently, if we can judge by his language, and the mission is quite obvious, liberation from the tyranny of Rome.

There are no RP on this passage.

LXX: v. 18, *soterí mou,* "my savior," a literal translation, which, in LXX, can only refer to God.

V: "My God Jesus," taking יִשְׁעִי , as a proper noun with first person singular suffix, from ישוע , the Hebrew name of Jesus.

S: ܦܪܘܩܝ , "my redeemer," literal, with no specific Messianic reference.

ZECHARIAH

H   3:8   Hear now, O Joshua, the High Priest, you and your friends that sit before you; for they are men that are a sign; for, behold, I will bring forth My servant the Branch.

J   Hear now, O Joshua, the High Priest, you and[141] your companions who sit before you, for they are men worthy of having miracles performed for them: Behold, I bring My servant, the Messiah, who is to be revealed.

MI: צֶמַח, "Branch."

LXX: Messianic tone. *'Anatolén,* "Sunrise."

V: Messianic, rendering צֶמַח as *Oriens,* "The Rising Sun," from LXX, which probably took it as the cognate Semitic root, "to shine."

S: Reworked, apparently, to conform to V: ܕܢܚܐ. LXX, V and S may have been influenced by the Targum. Cf. Psalms 72:5, H and T *infra* p. 115, also note III, 17.

Zech.

H   4:7   Who are you, O great mountain? Before Zerubbabel you
            shall be a plain; and he shall bring forward the top stone,
            with shouts of "Grace, grace to it."

J   Of what worth are you before Zerubbabel, you foolish king-
            dom?[142] Are you not like a plain? For He shall reveal His
            Messiah, whose name was called from the beginning, and
            he shall have dominion over all the kingdoms.

MI: הָאֶבֶן, "the stone," which is here used by the Targum for
the only time to adduce the Messianic. Cf. Matt. 21:42.

The great mountain is an empire that has foolishly oppressed the
Jewish people. Zerubbabel seems to be taken as the name of the
Messiah, for it is in comparison with him that the high mountain is
like a plain. In the course of the evolution of the Messiah idea
Zerubbabel was considered as a Messianic personality.[143]

In the RP, there is an interpretation of this verse entirely different
from what we have in the Targum.   הַר הַגָּדוֹל , "great mountain,"
which J takes as an oppressive empire, an adversary of the Messiah, is taken as the Messiah himself. "What are you, O great
mountain, (Zech. 4:7), this is the King Messiah, and why does he
call him 'great mountain?' For he is greater than the Patriarchs,"
etc. (Yalkut Shimeoni, *ad loc.,* and Pirke deR. Eliezer IX.)

Zech.

H   6:12   And you shall say unto him thus: "Thus says the Lord of Hosts, saying: Behold a man whose name is the Branch, and who shall grow up from his place, and build the temple of the Lord.

J   Say unto him: "Thus says the Lord of Hosts saying: Behold the man whose name is 'The Messiah.' He is destined to be revealed and to be anointed, and he shall build the Temple of the Lord.

H   6:13   And it is he who shall build the temple of the Lord; and he shall bear the majestic.splendor, and shall sit and rule upon his throne; and there shall be a priest by his throne; and the counsel of peace shall be between them both."

J   He shall build the Temple of the Lord, and he will bear the radiance,[144] and shall sit and rule upon his throne; and there shall be a high priest[145] on his throne, and there shall be a counsel of peace[146] betwen the two of them."

MI: צֶמַח, "Branch," in v. 12.

In v. 12, יִצְמָח, "he shall grow," is related to צֶמַח, "Branch," and is interpreted as the symbolic act which will make him the Messiah. In v. 13, הוֹד , "majestic splendor," is interpreted as radiance, possibly divine radiance.

The Messiah here is the one who will rebuild the Temple, basking in the glory of the divine. There will be an understanding between the political and the sacerdotal power, which is usually identified with Elijah, but not specifically so here.

RP: ". . . 'Behold a man whose name is Branch, and who shall grow up' (Zech. 6:12). This refers to the Messiah." Numbers Rabbah 18:21. ". . . from the tribe of Judah were descended Solomon, who built the first Temple, and Zerubbabel who built the second Temple; and from him will be descended the King Messiah, who will rebuild the Temple." Genesis Rabbah (NV), Soncino 97, p. 901.

LXX: Literal, but with Messianic overtones. צֶמַח is rendered by *'Anatolè.*

V: Ecce vir Oriens nomen ejus, "Behold a man whose name is *Oriens.*" Messianic.

S: Reworked to conform with *Oriens* of V.

Zechariah 9:9-10. These verses are rendered literally by the Targum, with no specific Messianic reference whatsoever, bearing out the contention that the humble, suffering, and dying Messiah was not acceptable to the Jewish mind.[147]

Zech.

H 10:4 Out of them shall come forth the corner-stone, out of them the stake, out of them the battle bow, out of them every master together.

J Out of him comes his king, out of him comes his Messiah, out of him comes his strength in battle, out of him shall grow all of his leaders as one.

MI: יָתֵד , "the stake," the only time we find this used as the proof-term for the Messiah, perhaps as the tent-peg, which supports the tent, a symbol of Torah.

J takes every phrase in this verse as metaphor, and gives his own interpretation of the meaning of each, accordingly.

There is no RP for this interpretation, and LXX, V, and S all render this passage literally.

SUMMARY OF TARGUM JONATHAN
TO THE PROPHETS

Targum Jonathan presents Messianic interpretations in the following passages: I Samuel 2:7-10, 35;[148] II Samuel 22:28-32; 23:1-5; I Kings 5:13; Isaiah 4:1-6; 9:5-6; 10:24-27; 11:1-16; 14:29-30; 16:1-5; 28:5-6; 42:1-9; 43:10; 52:13-53:12; Jeremiah 23:1-8; 30:8-11; 33:13-22, 25-26; Ezekiel 17:22-24; 34:20-31; 37:21-28; Hosea 2:2; 3:3-5; 14:5-8; Micah 4:8; 5:1-4; Habakkuk 3:17-18; Zechariah 3:8; 4:7; 6:12-13; 10:4.

Very striking is the fact that J abounds in eschatological material, so much so that there are not many chapters of the Latter Prophets, Ezekiel included, without an eschatological reference, and yet the Messianic references are so relatively few. J, like its counterpart O to the Pentateuch, is exceedingly sparing in its Messianism. Even Zech. 9:9 and Mal. 4:5 are not interpreted Messianically!

The Messianic exposition of J varies according to the prophet being interpreted, and according to the period and outlook of the Targumic interpreter. In First Isaiah, the Messiah is depicted as a symbol of peace and harmony in the world, as a righteous judge, as the champion of social justice. In Deutero-Isaiah, the Suffering Servant is recast by the Targumist into a glorious Messiah, who is not only the champion of justice, righteousness, and the Torah, but who is a warrior who despoils the enemies of his people and restores Jewish sovereignty. He also intercedes with God for the sins of his people, and brings them back to the right path, for he has the power to dispense personal reward and punishment. The emphasis in Jeremiah is on the ingathering of the exiles and the restoration of the genuine leadership of the Davidic dynasty, with the Messiah representing the indestructible, eternal covenant between God and David. In Ezekiel the Targum approaches the subject of Messianism with great reluctance, avoiding completely the use of ordinary Targumic Messianic terminology. In Hosea, the Messianic emphasis is on repentance, in Micah it is on security, and in Zechariah, on the rebuilding of the Temple.

It is apparent that no generalizations can be made, because there are too many variations. Each passage must be judged by itself on its own merits. The Targum reflects too many minds and too many points of view. In this respect, it is a mirror of the free expression of thought which prevailed in the rabbinic period of which it is a product. It gives voice to some of the ideas that are found in other rabbinic sources, but it also demonstrates its own independence of thought and its own exegetical genius. But, despite the absence of unanimity of interpretation regarding detail, there is a definitely unified and coherent thread of Messianic thought that stretches from beginning to end of the Targum's rendering of the Prophets.

CHAPTER III

THE MESSIANIC EXEGESIS OF THE TARGUM TO THE HAGIOGRAPHA

Unlike the Pentateuch and the Prophets, the Hagiographa was not read as a part of the regular Sabbath service in the synagogue. Consequently, there arose no official Targum to the Hagiographa bearing the stamp of approval and authority. The Five Megillot, however, did become an integral part of the holiday liturgy, and Aramaic renderings did evolve for all the books of the Hagiographa except Daniel and Ezra-Nehemiah. These, however, are heterogeneous; they are not all of the same authorship, nor do they have the same characteristics or delineations, but they differ, sometimes extremely.

The precise dates of these various Targumim have not been ascertained. However, it is known that some of these were extant at an early period.[1] On the other hand, there is evidence that some of these Targumim contain material stemming from a very late period in Jewish history.[2]

In the Rabbinic Bibles these Targumim are simply designated "Targum," without any other appellation or distinguishing qualifications such as we find on the Targumim to the other sections of the Scriptures, and we indicate it here by the symbol T. The critical editions of Lagarde and Sperber IV A (without Psalms, Proverbs, and Job, the latter two having no Messianic references in any case) were compared with the Warsaw edition of the Rabbinic Bible.

PSALMS

Psalm 2, which is one of the Psalms generally regarded as Messianic,[3] is of doubtful Messianic interpretation in the Targum. Verse 2 is translated thus: "Kings of earth stand up, and rulers have banded together to rebel against the Lord, and to quarrel with His anointed." The general tone of the Targumic rendering of the entire Psalm is not the usually strong Messianic tone. Verse 7 is translated, "I will tell the decree of the Lord: He said, 'You are as dear to Me as a son is to a father; you are as meritorious as though I had created you this day.' "[4]

Rashi, *ad loc.*, interprets the Psalm as referring to David, in the context of II Sam. 5:17 ff. Ibn Ezra, *ad loc.*, prefers to take it with reference to David, but would interpret it Messianically as a second choice. The Targum's version does not appear to be Messianic.

Ps.

H 18:28[5]   For Thou, a humble people dost Thou deliver; and the haughty eyes Thou dost bring low.

T   For Thou, Thou shalt in the future deliver the people of the house of Israel, who are humbled[6] among the nations in the Dispersion, and with Thy Memra Thou shalt bring low the mighty nations who lord over them.

H 18:29   Verily, Thou dost light my lamp, the Lord my God will illumine my darkness.

T   For Thou shalt light up the lamp of Israel which is flickering[7] in the Dispersion, for Thou, art the master of the light of Israel. The Lord my God will bring me out of the darkness into the light. He will comfort me with the consolation of the world which is destined to come for the righteous.

H 18:30   Truly, by Thee I can run with a troop, and by my God I can scale a wall.

T   For by Thy Memra I shall raise a mighty army, and by the Memra of my God I shall conquer fortified cities.

H 18:31   The God, His way is perfect, the word of the Lord is proven, He is the shield of all who take refuge in Him.

T   God, His way is perfect; the Torah of the Lord is choice; He is the shield of all who trust in Him.

H 18:32   Verily, who is God other than the Lord, and who is a rock, except our God?

T   For, in consequence of the miracle and the deliverance which Thou shalt perform for Thy Messiah and for the remnant of Thy people who remain, all peoples, nations, and tongues shall confess, and say: "There is no God but the Lord," verily there is none besides Thee. And Thy people shall say, "There is none mighty, save our God."

This is a variation of J to II Sam. 22:28-32.[8] The rendering differs in some respects. It is somewhat more elaborate in vv. 28 and 29, and elsewhere uses slightly different language from J. On the whole it would seem that the Targumist to this passage had J and reworked it, even utilizing J's designation of משיחא, rather than מלכא משיחא .

A: لَا إِلَهَ إِلَّا ٱلرَّبُّ , la ilaha illa 'rrabbu, the Moslem article of faith with the substitution of "the Lord," for "Allah." [9]

Ps.

H	21:1	For the choirmaster, a Psalm of David.
T		For the singer, a Psalm of David.
H	21:2	O Lord, in Thy strength the king rejoices, and in Thy salvation how greatly he exults.
T		O Lord, the King Messiah shall be happy in Thy strength, and in Thy deliverance how greatly he shall rejoice.[10]
H	21:3	His heart's desire Thou hast given him, the request of his lips Thou hast not withheld. Selah.
T		Thou hast given him his soul's desire, and hast not withheld the expression of his lips, forever.[11]
H	21:4	Verily, Thou dost greet him with goodly blessings; Thou dost set upon his head a crown of fine gold.
T		For Thou shalt meet him with goodly blessings; Thou shalt place upon his head a crown of pure gold.
H	21:5	Life he asked of Thee: Thou hast given it to him, length of days forever and ever.
T		Eternal life he asked of Thee; Thou hast given it to him, length of days forever and ever.
H	21:6	Great is his glory by Thy salvation; majesty and splendor Thou dost bestow upon him.
T		Great is his glory through Thy deliverance; praise and splendor shalt Thou bestow upon him.
H	21:7	Verily, Thou dost render him blessings forever, Thou dost gladden him.
T		For Thou shalt bestow upon him blessings forever; Thou shalt make him rejoice with a joy which comes from Thee.
H	21:8	For the king trusts in the Lord, and by the loving kindness of the Most High he shall not be moved.
T		For the King Messiah trusts in the Lord, and through the loving kindness of the Most High he shall not be moved.

MI: מֶלֶךְ , "king," in vv. 2 and 8.

The rendering is virtually literal, apart from the interpretation of "king" as "King Messiah," and "life," in v. 5 as "eternal life." The belief that the Messiah would live eternally was widespread, and is intimately linked with the resurrection of the dead, which was to be effected by Elijah even before the advent of the Messiah, and with the Last Judgment, which would usher in the unending age of righteousness. The idea that the Messiah would live for a limited time only, and then die, while found in 4 Esdras, 7:28-29, was not generally accepted in Jewish thought. As a matter of fact, it was this very reluctance to assign death to the Messiah, and the historical events in which Messianic pretenders met death, that gave rise to the doctrine of the Ephraimite Messiah, who would precede the real Messiah and meet death in battle.[12] But the Davidic Messiah would possess eternal life.[13] Or, at the very least, would live for a millenium.[14]

Here the Messiah is the symbol of the security, the joy, and the tranquillity which result from faith in God.

RP: In the rabbinic sources this Psalm is usually viewed as Messianic. Sukkah 52a; Yalkut Shimeoni *ad loc.* Exodus Rabbah 8:1 expresses the thought that God will place His own crown on the head of the Messiah.

LXX, V, and *S* all translate literally. V has a Christological superscription, however.

Ps.

H 45:1 For the Leader; upon Shoshannim; [a Psalm] of the sons of Korah. Maskil. A Song of loves.

T For the singer. Dedicated to the members of the Sanhedrin of Moses. Spoken through prophecy by the Sons of Korah: goodly wisdom, praise, and thanksgiving.

H 45:2 My heart overflows with a goodly matter; I say: My work is for the king; my tongue is the pen of a ready scribe.

T My heart seeks to utter something good. I say: My doings are for the King. My mind expresses itself[15] like the pen of the trained scribe.

H 45:3 You are fairer than the children of men; grace is poured upon your lips; therefore God has blessed you forever.

T Your beauty, O King Messiah, surpasses that of ordinary men. The spirit of prophecy has been bestowed upon your lips; therefore, the Lord has blessed you forever.

H 45:4 Gird your sword upon your thigh, O mighty one, your glory and your majesty.

T Gird your sword upon your thigh, O mighty one;[16] it is your glory and your splendor.

H 45:5 And in your majesty prosper, ride on, in behalf of truth and meekness and righteousness; and let your right hand teach you wondrous things.

T And your splendor is great. Because of this you shall ride victoriously on the steeds of the kingdom in behalf of[17] faith, truth, humility, and righteousness. And the Lord shall teach you to perform awesome deeds with your right hand.

H 45:6 Your arrows are sharp—peoples fall under you; into the heart of the king's enemies.

T Your arrows are drawn;[18] nations shall fall under you. And your arrows[19] shall be sent into the heart of the King's enemies.

H   45:7   Your divine throne is forever and ever; a scepter of equity is the scepter of your kingdom.

T   Thy throne of glory, O Lord, endures forever and ever; a scepter of righteousness is the scepter of Thy Kingdom.

H   45:8   You have loved righteousness, and hated wickedness; therefore God, your God, has anointed you with the oil of gladness above your fellows.

T   Because you love righteousness and hate evil, because of this the Lord your God has anointed you with the oil of gladness more than your companion.

H   45:9   Myrrh and aloes, and cassia are all your garments; out of ivory palaces stringed instruments have made you glad.

T   Pure myrrh and aloes and cassia perfume all your garments. Out of palaces inlaid with ivory from the land of Minni[20] they shall gladden you.

H   45:10   Kings' daughters are among your favorites; at your right hand stands the queen in gold of Ophir.

T   The districts of the kingdom come forward to greet you and to honor you when the scroll of the Torah is placed at your right, inscribed with pure gold of Ophir.[21]

H   45:11   Hearken, O daughter and consider, and incline your ear; forget your own people and your father's house.

T   Hear, O congregation of Israel, the instruction of his mouth and observe the extent of his deeds. Let your ear attend to the words of the Torah, forget the evil deeds of the wicked of your people, and the house of idolatry where you served, the house of your fathers.

H   45:12   So shall the king desire your beauty; for he is your lord; and do homage unto him.

T   And then the King will desire your beauty, for He is your master and you must bow to Him.

H   45:13   And the daughter of Tyre, with a gift, shall entreat your favor; the richest of the people.

T   The inhabitants of the city of Tyre shall come with an offering; the rich people of the nations shall seek your presence at your Temple.

H 45:14   All glorious is the king's daughter within the palace; her raiment is wrought with gold.

T   All the finest personal possessions from the district treasuries of kings, hidden within, shall be brought to the priests, whose vestments are woven of pure gold.

H 45:15   She shall be led unto the king on richly woven stuff; the virgins her companions in her train being brought unto you.

T   In embroidered vestments they shall offer their sacrifices before the King of the world; and the rest of their fellows, who are scattered among the nations shall be brought in to you, rejoicing, at Jerusalem.

H 45:16   They shall be led with gladness and rejoicing. They shall enter into the king's palace.

T   They shall be brought in with joy and praises, and they shall enter the palace of the Eternal King.

H 45:17   Instead of your fathers shall be your sons, whom you shall make princes in all the land.

T   In the place of your fathers your sons shall be righteous; you shall appoint them princes in all the land.

H 45:18   I will make your name to be remembered in every generation; therefore shall the peoples praise you forever and ever.

T   At that time you shall say: "Let us remember Thy name in every generation." Because of this, the people who become proselytes shall praise Thy name forever and ever.

MI: The Messianic exegesis of the Targumist in this Psalm is interesting. It is adduced from the phrase מְשָׁחֲךָ אֱלֹהִים , "God has anointed you," v. 8, and a vague contextual intimation, and is introduced in v. 3. The Hebrew מֶלֶךְ, "king," in vv. 2, 6, 12, 15, and 16, which we would expect to be a normal MI for the Targum, is understood as God, and in v. 14 is even taken in the temporal sense and is applied to those kings of the nations who will pay tribute to the Temple in Jerusalem in Messianic times. The inter- weaving of the references to God, the Messiah, and Israel is skillful, if difficult to follow at times.

The exegesis generally follows the Hebrew rather closely, though it is paraphrastic and explanatory here and there. The superscription in v. 1, dedicates this to the members of the Sanhedrin of Moses. Rashi, *ad loc.*, interprets the entire Psalm as having reference to the sages who spend their lives in the study of Torah. Mention of the scribe in v. 2 lends itself readily to such an interpretation. The Targumic explanation of שֵׁגָל , "queen," in v. 10, is "Torah"; and the ideal of Torah is injected into v. 11, in explanation of שִׁמְעִי בַת , "hear, O daughter," with בַת understood as the congregation of Israel. Something akin to Torah is expounded in v. 5 on וְתוֹרְךָ , "and let it teach," which the Targum takes as the instruction of God, and which S reads וְתוֹרָתְךָ , "and your Torah." In fact the Messiah is depicted as the champion of God, the Torah, and the gentler virtues that go with learning and culture, such as prophecy, v. 3, and faith, truth, humility, and righteousness, v. 5;[22] even the martian language of vv. 4 and 6 is interpreted in these terms; the dedication to the Sanhedrin, to men of learning and culture, thus becomes intelligible, and the seeming incongruity between the dedication and the body of the Psalm is thus cleared away. In v. 8b the Targum reads the singular מֵחַבְרֶךְ , "your companion," for the Masoretic מֵחַבְרֶיךָ , "your companions." Who this companion might be is not explained. It may possibly refer to the Messiah son of Joseph, the Ephraimite Messiah, but this is only conjecture. Ibn Ezra, *ad loc.*, accepting the Masoretic reading, says: "If the Psalm refers to David then מֵחַבְרֶיךָ refers to Saul; and if (the Psalm) is about the Messiah, then (the word) refers to the other pious men of his generation."

RP: Rabbinic views of this Psalm are not Messianic. Some opinions are that it refers to scholars and those who study Torah,

Shabbat 63b, and some maintain that the subject is Abraham, Yalkut Shimeoni, *ad loc.;* Genesis Rabbah 59:6.

LXX, V, and *S* translate literally. V has a Christological superscription. The Targum's influence can be seen in Brigg's paradox,[23] that though this Psalm was occasioned by Joram's marriage to Athaliah, it still mirrors the bridal ,of the Messiah with the nations.

Ps.

H 61:7[24] Mayest Thou add days unto the king's days! May his years be as generation upon generation.

T Days in addition to the days of the World-to-Come[25] are the days of the King Messiah; Thou shalt increase his years as the generations of this world and the generations of the World-to-Come.

H 61:8 May he be enthroned forever before God! Appoint mercy and truth, that they may preserve him.

T He shall dwell forever before the Lord; goodness and truth from the Master of the world shall guard him.

H 61:9 So will I sing praise unto Thy name forever, that I may daily perform my vows.

T Therefore I shall praise Thy name forever, when I fulfil my vows on the day of Israel's deliverance, and on the day that the King Messiah is anointed king.

MI: מֶלֶךְ , "king," in v. 7.

The Targum differs from the Masorah in its division of v. 7, reading תוֹסִיף , "Thou shalt increase," in 7b rather than 7a. It feels 7a to be laconic and adds the complement, "the days of the World-to-Come." The expression דֹר וָדֹר , "from generation to generation," lends itself to the interpretation of both worlds. In v. 8 the Targum reads מִן, "from," for the Masoretic מַן, "appoint." This, too, is laconic and·is filled in. In v. 9 יוֹם יוֹם , "day by day," suggests two days, the day of Israel's deliverance and the day of the anointing of the Messiah.

The Targumic view is that the Messiah will live forever under God's protection. Likewise there is expressed the thought here that David, the author of this Psalm, will be resurrected in time to see both the anointing of his descendant as the Messiah, and the deliverance of Israel, which will precede that event.

RP: Pirke deR. Eliezer XVIII follows the Messianic interpretation of these verses by the Targum. The versions render them literally. V, however, carries a Messianic heading.

Ps.

H 72:1 A Psalm of Solomon. Give the king Thy judgments, O God, and Thy righteousness unto the king's son.

T By the hand of Solomon, spoken through prophecy. O God, give the King Messiah the laws[26] of Thy justice, and Thy righteousness to the son of King David.

H 72:2 That he may judge Thy people with righteousness, and Thy poor with justice.

T He shall judge Thy people with righteousness, and Thy poor with a law of justice.

H 72:3 Let the mountains bear peace to the people, and the hills, through righteousness.

T Those who dwell on the mountains shall bring peace to the house of Israel, and the hills with merit.[27]

H 72:4 May he judge the poor of the people, and save the children of the needy, and crush the oppressor.

T He shall judge the poor of the people, he shall deliver the unfortunate, and crush the man who oppresses.

H 72:5 They shall fear Thee while the sun endures, and so long as the moon, throughout all generations.

T They shall worship Thee with the rising of the sun, and they shall pray to Thee by the light[28] of the moon throughout all generations.

H 72:6 May he come down like rain upon the mown grass, as showers that water the earth.

T He shall come down like a welcome rain on grass shorn away by locusts, like drops of late rain that moisten the grass of the earth.

H 72:7 Iₙ his days let the righteous flourish, and abundance of peace, till the moon be no more.

T The righteous shall be numerous in his day, and peace shall abound, until those who worship the moon shall be destroyed.

H   72:8   May he have dominion from sea to sea, and from the River unto the ends of the earth.

T   He shall have dominion from one side of the Mediterranean[29] to the other, and from the Euphrates to the ends of the earth.

H   72:9   Let them that dwell in the wilderness bow before him; and his enemies lick the dust.

T   Governors of provinces shall bow down before him, and his enemies shall lick the dust.

H   72:10   The kings of Tarshish and of the isles shall render tribute; the kings of Sheba and Seba shall offer gifts.

T   The kings of Tarsus and the isles of Ocean[30] shall return tribute, the kings of Sheba and Seba shall bring a gift.

H   72:11   And all kings shall prostrate themselves before him; all nations shall serve him.

T   All kings shall bow down to him, all nations shall become subject to him.

H   72:12   For he will deliver the needy when he cries; the poor also, and him that has no helper.

T   For he shall deliver the needy when he asks for help, and the poor, and him who has no helper.

H   72:13   He will have pity on the poor and needy, and the souls of the needy he will save.

T   He shall have pity on the poor and the needy, and shall save the lives of the unfortunate.

H   72:14   He will redeem their soul from oppression and violence, and precious will their blood be in his sight.

T   From persecution and violence he shall save their lives, and their blood shall be precious to him.

H   72:15   May he live, and be given of the gold of Sheba, may he pray for him continually, may he bless him all the day.

T He shall live, and give the poor[31] of the gold which they shall bring him from Sheba, so that he[31] shall always pray for him and bless him all the day long.

H 72:16 May there be a rich cornfield in the land upon the top of the mountains; may his fruit rustle like Lebanon; and may they blossom out of the city like grass of the earth.

T May there be an abundance of bread in the land; on the mountain tops may its fruit shake like Lebanon; and may they[32] sprout from the city of Jerusalem like the grass of the earth.

H 72:17 May his name endure forever; may his name be continued as long as the sun; may men also bless themselves by him; may all nations invoke happiness upon him.

T May his name be remembered forever, his name which was made ready even before the sun came into being. By his merit all nations shall be blessed. and they shall say: "It is well with him."

H 72:18 Blessed be the Lord God, the God of Israel, who alone does wondrous things.

T Blessed is the Lord God, the God of Israel, who alone does great wonders.

H 72:19 And blessed be His glorious name forever; and let the whole earth be filled with His glory. Amen and Amen.

T And blessed be His glorious name forever. And may the whole earth be filled with the effulgence of His glory. Amen and Amen.

H 72:20 The prayers of David, the son of Jesse, are ended.

T The prayers of David, the son of Jesse, are ended.

MI: לְמֶלֶךְ , "to the king," and לִבֶן מֶלֶךְ , "to the son of the king," v. 1.

In v. 1, the Targum understands לִשְׁלֹמֹה as "by Solomon," meaning that he was the author, not the subject, of the Psalm. The first reference to "king" is to the Messiah; the second reference is to David, whose offspring is the Messiah. The entire Psalm is taken Messianically.

In v. 3, "mountains" is explained as "those who dwell on mountains," but there is no such explanation for "hills."

The "oppressor" in v. 4 is the individual, the man who oppresses his fellowman, not an oppressing nation, as it might be interpreted in a Messianic context.

Verse 5 is interpreted as a reference to the daily morning and evening prayers of Jewish worship.

In v. 6, the Targumist takes the trouble to clarify the expression גֵּז , "shorn grass"; it is not grass that has been mown by man, but chewed up by locusts, making its regrowth more difficult, and making the rain doubly welcome.

"The moon," v. 7, is explained as idolatrous moon-worship.

"From sea to sea," v. 8, from one side of the Mediterranean to the other. "The River," the Euphrates, a usual Biblical usage.

In v. 9 צִיִּים is rendered "governors of provinces," perhaps because the Hebrew means "ships" or "wilderness," either of which suggests distant or outlying points.

There is a geographic elaboration on "isles," v. 10, meaning the isles of Ocean, the remotest outposts.

The thought which is prevalent in rabbinic Judaism, of the pre-existence of the name of the Messiah,[33] is again expressed in v. 17.

The Messianic picture is that of a supreme ruler who will be the champion of social justice in his own land, whose reign will be universal over the world, in whose time idolatry will be supplanted by the worship of God, to whom nations will pay tribute, which he will distribute equitably as a solution to the problem of poverty and need.

RP: "Another interpretation: 'Give the king Thy judgments' (Ps. 72:1), this refers to the King Messiah." Yalkut Shimeoni, *ad loc.* The dominant rabbinic opinion is that this Psalm generally, and specific verses, are Messianic. As a matter of record, the Masoretic *Q're* יִנּוֹן , "Yinnon," in v. 17 is held to be the name of the Messiah by one school of thought.[34]

LXX, V, and *S* all translate literally, but the latter two bear Messianic superscriptions.

Ps.

H 80:15[35]   O God of hosts, return, we beseech Thee; look from heaven, and behold, and be mindful of this vine,

T   O God of hosts, turn now, look down[36] from heaven and
see, and remember this vine in mercy,

H 80:16   And of the stock which Thy right hand has planted, and
the branch that Thou hast made strong for Thyself.

T   And the stock which Thy right hand[37] has planted and upon
the King Messiah whom Thou hast made strong for Thy-
self.

H 80:17   It is burned with fire, it is cut down; they perish at the
rebuke of Thy countenance.

T   It[38] is burned with fire and crumbled. May they perish by
Thy wrath.

H 80:18   Let Thy hand be upon the man of Thy right hand, upon
the son of man whom Thou hast made strong for Thyself.

T   Let Thy hand be upon the man whom Thou hast established
with Thy right hand, upon the son of man[39] whom Thou
hast made strong for Thyself.

MI: בֵּן , v. 16.

The Hebrew text of v. 16 is difficult, and has caused much concern among exegetes. Verse 18 appears to be a gloss in explanation
of v. 16, with Messianic emphasis, but "son of man" in v. 18 is
rendered literally by the Targum, and as a strictly human reference.
This is the only instance in which the Targum interprets בֵּן Messianically. At first glance this may appear to be an incongruity,
not only for the Targum, but for Jewish Messianism generally,
since it would appear that the Targum takes the Messiah to be the
son of God, which is much too anthropomorphic and Christological
to be acceptable in Jewish exegesis. There is no RP for this interpretation of this verse, either in the earlier rabbinic sources or in
later Jewish commentaries. Rashi, Ibn Ezra, *et al,* carefully steer
clear of any Messianic interpretation. Yet it is clear and unmistak-

able in the Targum, found both in the critical and uncritical editions. It has never been censored or deleted, in spite of its precarious position, theologically. Although it sounds Christological, almost as though it had been injected by a Christian exegete, it is probably Jewish to the core, a link in the unbroken chain of Jewish Messianic tradition. For, in this Hebrew context בֵּן cannot mean "son." It parallels וְכַנָּה , "the stock," which God's right hand planted and גֶּפֶן , "vine," in vv. 9 and 15, which represents Israel. What it is taken to mean, then, is "branch," as it does in a similar poetic expression in Gen. 49:22: בֵּן פֹּרָת יוֹסֵף , "Joseph is a fruitful branch." It is equated with צֶמַח , a very popular MI in the Targum, and generally in the Hebrew Scriptures.

This is another example of the remarkable phenomenon of Targumic transmission. We have seen that the Targum to Ezekiel has come down without specific Messianic designation, without gloss or interpolation, even where the text calls for such.[40] The present passage in the Targum represents the opposite, a case of Messianic interpretation which seems out of place, both theologically and exegetically, and yet has been preserved intact, without modification or deletion.

  LXX: ". . . and upon the son of man."
  V: ". . . and upon the son of man."
  S: ". . . and to the son of man."

Ps.

H   89:51   Remember, O Lord, the taunt of Thy servants; how I do bear in my bosom the insults of so many peoples,

T   Remember, O Lord, the revilement of Thy servant; I bore in my bosom all the blasphemies of many nations,

H   89:52   Wherewith Thine enemies have taunted, O Lord, wherewith they have taunted the footsteps of Thine anointed.

T   With which Thy enemies have scoffed, O Lord, with which they have scoffed at the delay of the footsteps of Thy Messiah, O Lord.

MI: מְשִׁיחֶךָ , "Thy anointed," v. 52.

In v. 51 the Targum supplies "blasphemies," for the text is laconic. In v. 52, it supplies "delay," in keeping with the idea that the enemies cannot scoff at the Messiah himself, since he has not yet come, but rather they scoff at the fact that the Jewish people is looking for him and he is delayed; they laugh at the very thought of his coming at all.

RP: "R. Jannai said: If you see one generation after another cursing and blaspheming, look for the footsteps of the King Messiah, as it is said, 'Wherewith Thy enemies have taunted, etc.' (Ps. 89:52)." Song of Songs Rabbah 2:13.

V: Christi tui, definitely in line with the Targum.

Psalm 110, which is taken Messianically by Christian exegetes,[41] is referred specifically to David by the Targum: "A Psalm by the hand of David. The Lord said by His Memra that He would make me the ruler of all Israel. However, He said to me: 'Sit and wait until Saul, who is of the tribe of Benjamin, dies, so that one kingdom may not crowd out the other; after that I will make your enemies your footstool.'"

The Targum interprets שֵׁב לִימִינִי , "sit at My right hand" as "sit (wait) for the Benjamite (Saul)."

The other rabbinic sources apply this Psalm to Abraham, Sanhedrin 108b, as does Rashi, *ad loc.* Ibn Ezra, *ad loc.,* applies it to David.

Ps.

H 132:10   For Thy servant David's sake turn not away the face of Thine anointed.

T   Because of the merit of David, Thy servant, do not turn away the face of Solomon, Thy anointed one, when he brings up the ark through the middle of the gates.[42]

H 132:11   The Lord swore unto David in truth; He will not turn back from it: "Of the fruit of your body will I set upon your throne.

T   The Lord swore to David in faithfulness and from which He will not turn back: "Of the child of your body, I will place a king upon your throne.

H 132:12   If your children keep My covenant and My testimony that I shall teach them, their children also forever shall sit upon your throne.

T   If your sons keep My covenant and My testimonies which I shall teach them, also their sons forever shall sit upon your throne.

H 132:13   For the Lord has chosen Zion; He has desired it for His habitation.

T   For the Lord has chosen Zion; He has desired her for His dwelling place.

H 132:14   This is My resting place forever; here will I dwell, for I have desired it.

T   This is the resting place of My Shekinah forever; here I will dwell, for I have desired her.

H 132:15   I will abundantly bless her provision; I will give her needy bread in plenty.

T   I will surely bless her provision, and her poor shall be satisfied with bread.

H 132:16   Her priests also will I clothe with salvation, and her saints shall shout for joy.

T   Her priests I will clothe with garments of salvation, and her pious ones shall surely sing praises.

H 132:17   There will I make a horn to sprout for David, there have
            I prepared a lamp for My anointed.

T   There I will make sprout a glorious king for the house
            of David; I have prepared a lamp for My Messiah.

H 132:18   His enemies will I clothe with shame, but upon himself
            shall his crown shine."

T   His enemies I will clothe with garments of shame, but upon
            him his crown shall glitter."

MI: לִמְשִׁיחִי , "for My anointed," v. 17.

Verse 10 is included in this selection to demonstrate the nature
of the Targum's Messianic exegesis. The word for "anointed one"
in v. 10 and for "My Messiah," in v. 17 are the same, משיחא ,
differing only in the personal suffixes. Both are translations of the
same Hebrew word. Yet, the Targum says pointedly that the
reference in v. 10 is to Solomon, and not Messianic in the sense
in which we have defined Messianism, while content and context
would indicate that the reference in v. 17 is probably Messianic.
An anointed one is not necessarily the Messiah. This is true not
only in this instance, but in Is. 45:1, with reference to Cyrus, and
elsewhere.[43]

In v. 10, the Targum explains that the anointed one in question
is Solomon, and the request for favor is for the occasion of the
dedication of the Temple.

Verses 16 and 18, "garments," is supplied as the object of
"clothe."

Verse 17, "horn" is interpreted as "glorious king."

RP: "R. Hanin said: By virtue of the merit of causing a lamp
to burn continually (Lev. 24:2) you will be worthy to welcome
the lamp of the King Messiah. What is the reason? Because it
says, 'There I will make a horn to sprout for David, etc.' (Ps.
132:17)." Leviticus Rabbah 31:11.

The other versions render this passage literally, without Messianic interpretation.

SONG OF SONGS

H   1:8   If you know not, O you among women, go your way forth by the footsteps of the flock, and feed your kids, besides the shepherds' tents.

T   Said the Holy One, blessed be He, to Moses the Prophet: If they wish to wipe out[44] the Dispersion, the congregation, which is likened to a beautiful maiden, and so that I Myself may love her, let her walk in the ways of the righteous, and let her arrange[45] her prayer-service according to her prayer-leaders and the leaders of her generation; and let her teach her children, who are comparable to kids, to go to the synagogue and to the school, and by the merit thereof they shall be provided for in the Dispersion until the time when I send the King Messiah, who shall lead them gently to their tents, that is, the Temple which David and Solomon, the shepherds of Israel, have built[46] for them.

There is no specific MI in the text. The Targum to the Song of Songs is in reality a Midrashic commentary. It takes its cues from the text, but the free flight of fancy is virtually without limit. In this passage, the Messianic interpretation may have been suggested by the pastoral imagery and the figure of the shepherds.

Moses comes into the picture here, in line with the Targum's exposition of the beginning of Song of Songs as a metaphorical presentation of Hebrew history. In the previous verse, the Targumist has God revealing to Moses, who is about to die, that Israel will sin and be carried off into Exile among the descendants of Esau and Ishmael.[47] In this verse, Moses is given insight into the secret of survival for Israel among the nations, leading to the deliverance.

Exegetically, "beautiful among women," is the congregation of Israel; "tracks of the flock" is the ways of the righteous; "feed your kids" is teach your children; "tents" is Temple; and "shepherds" refers to David and Solomon, in the context of their historical roles.

There are no RP to this verse, and the other versions have no Messianic reference.

SS

H   1:17   The beams of our houses are cedars, and our panels are cypresses.

T   Said Solomon, the Prophet: How beautiful is the Temple of the Lord which was built by my hands of cedar trees. But even more beautiful shall be the Temple, which is destined to be built in the days of the King Messiah, the beams of which shall be of cedars from the Garden of Eden, and the joists of which shall be of cypress, teak and pine.

The MI is uncertain. It may be that the Messianic is adduced from אֲרָזִים , "cedars," associated with Ezek. 17:22, but this is mere conjecture. It is probably suggested by the plural בָּתֵּינוּ , "our houses," which evokes thoughts of another Temple, in Messianic times.

There is no RP and the other versions render the passage literally.

SS

H   4:5   Your two breasts are like two fawns, that are twins of a
          gazelle, which feed among the lilies.

T   Your two deliverers who are destined to deliver you, the
          Messiah the son of David and the Messiah the son of
          Ephraim, are like Moses and Aaron, the sons of Jochebed,
          who are likened to two fawns, twins of a gazelle; who, by
          their merit, shepherded the people of Israel in the wilder-
          ness for forty years, supplying them with manna, fattened
          fowl, and with the water of the well of Miriam.

MI: הָרֹעִים , understood in the sense of shepherds, leaders, and
שָׁדַיִךְ , "your breasts."

In other rabbinic sources this verse is interpreted as applying to
Moses and Aaron, whose beauty, glory and nourishing power to
Israel are like the breasts of a woman, and who were regarded as
twins, i.e., equals in Torah.[48] The Targumist picks up the theme,
uses it, and carries it farther, into the realm of the Messianic, comparing the two Messiahs to Moses and Aaron.

There are no RP. The other versions are literal.

SS

H   7:4   Your two breasts are like two fawns that are twins of a gazelle.

T   Your two deliverers who are destined to deliver you, the Messiah the son of David and the Messiah the son of Ephraim, are like Moses and Aaron, the sons of Jochebed, who are likened to two fawns, twins of a gazelle.

The Hebrew is identical with 4:5a, but omits 5b. The Targumic rendering of this verse omits the explanatory note about Moses and Aaron found in 4:5b.

SS

H   7:12   Come, my beloved, let us go forth into the field; let us lodge in the villages.

T   When the people of the house of Israel sinned, the Lord exiled them to the land of Seir, the field of Edom.[49] Said the congregation of Israel: "O Master of all the world, please accept the prayer which I offer before Thee in the midst of the Dispersion and in the provinces of the nations."

H   7:13   Let us get up early to the vineyards; let us see whether the vine has budded, whether the vine-blossom be opened, and the pomegranates be in flower; there will I give you my love.

T   Say the children of Israel one to another: "Let us arise early in the morning and go to the synagogue and to the house of study, and let us search the books of the Torah, and let us see if the time has come for the deliverance of the people of the house of Israel, who are likened to a vine, to be delivered from their Dispersion. And let us inquire of the wise men if the merit of the righteous who are likened to the pomegranate[50] has been revealed by the Lord, whether the End[51] has arrived, to go up to Jerusalem, there to give praise unto the God of Heaven, and to offer up the burnt offerings and the holy sacrifices."

H   7:14   The mandrakes give forth fragrance, and at our doors are all precious fruits, new and old, which I have laid up for you, O my beloved.

T   And when it shall be the will of the Lord to deliver His people from the Dispersion,[52] He shall say[53] to the King Messiah: "Already the time of the End[51] of the Dispersion has been fulfilled. The merit of the righteous is as fragrant[54] to Me as the fragrance of spices.[55] And the sages of the generation[56] are gathered at the gates of the academy engaging in scholarly[57] discourse and in words of Torah. Arise, now, and accept the kingdom which I have stored away for you."[58]

SS

H 8:1 O that you were as my brother, who nursed at the breasts of my mother! If I should find you outside, I would kiss you, and none would despise me.

T And at that time the King Messiah will be revealed to the congregation of Israel. The children of Israel shall say to him: "Come, be a brother to us, and let us go up to Jerusalem and imbibe the explanations[59] of the Torah with you as a suckling child sucks the breasts of its mother. For, during the time that I wandered outside of my land, when I would remember the name of the great God and would sacrifice myself for His[60] Godhead, even the nations of the earth did not despise me.

H 8:2 I would lead you, and bring you into my mother's house, that you might instruct me. I would cause you to drink of spiced wine, of the juice of my pomegranate.

T I will conduct you, O King Messiah,[61] and take you into my Temple, that you may teach me to fear the Lord and to walk in His way. There we will partake of the feast of Leviathan, and we will drink the old wine which has been concealed in its grapes from the day when the world was created, and from pomegranates, the fruit made ready for the righteous in the Garden of Eden."

H 8:3 His left hand should be under my head, and his right hand should embrace me.

T Says the congregation of Israel: "I am the chosen of all peoples in that I bind the phylacteries upon my left arm and upon my forehead, and fasten a mezuzah on the upper third of the right side of the doorpost, so that the demons are powerless to injure me." [62]

H 8:4 I adjure you, O daughters of Jerusalem: Why should you awaken, or stir up love, until it please?

T The King Messiah shall say: "I adjure you, O my[63] people, house of Israel! Why do you contend with the nations of the earth in order to get out of the Dispersion,[64] and why do you rebel against the armed might of Gog and Magog?

> Would that you might wait but a little longer, until the nations who have gone up to wage war against Jerusalem are destroyed, and after that the Master of the world shall remember for your sake the love of the righteous, and it shall be His will to deliver you."

In this passage, likewise, it is impossible to detect any MI. The exegetical style is that of the Midrashic commentary, built up from a word here and there in the text. This is a good demonstration of the rabbinic idea that the Song of Songs is an allegorical discourse, primarily between God and Israel,[65] which is evident elsewhere in the Targum; here the Messiah is also introduced as a participant in the discourse.[66]

Reflected in the above passage are several matters pertaining to Messianism. Verse 7:13 indicates a trend that never was entirely checked, the tendency to look for the date of the advent of the Messiah in Holy Scriptures. Verse 14 intimates that the date will remain unknown except to God, and when the appointed time arrives, God will issue instructions to the Messiah; the date apparently will be contingent upon righteous deeds, which find their source and their strength in a knowledge and discussion of Torah. This is further elaborated on in 8:1, which intimates that even after the exiles return to their land an understanding of the Torah will be necessary in the Messianic age, no less for the Messiah than for Israel.

Reference to the kingdom which God had stored away in 7:14 pertains to its divine origin and plan, not to any pre-mundane existence.

In 8:2, the feast of Leviathan is introduced. In the apocalypses Leviathan and Behemoth are mentioned, with intimations of their Messianic purpose.[67] In rabbinic thought they assume greater proportions in later legends, as the food of the Messianic banquet, preserved from the fifth day.[68] The special Messianic elixir, wine preserved in its grapes since Creation, is also mentioned in the Talmud.[69] That the pomegranate will be food for the righteous in Paradise, or that they will drink of its juice, is a novel creation in Jewish legend by the author of this Targum,[70] probably suggested by the Hebrew text itself in 8:2. The only idea that even remotely resembles it in RP is the statement that in the Messianic age God would make Israel like a park of pomegranates,[71] based on the text of Song of Songs 4:13.

Verse 8:3 is interesting in that it clarifies, to some extent, the Jewish idea of a chosen people, chosen for greater duty and performance of divine injunctions, which carries with it a certain amount of protection from harm.

Verse 8:4 sounds a Messianic note that remains influential in some quarters to this day. Deliverance must be a divine act, not human, and even the Messiah is only a symbol. The Jewish people is not to strive for victory and vindication by itself, but to wait for divine intervention. An extreme Orthodox wing of Judaism to this day is opposed to the modern Zionist ideal on these grounds.

The other versions render this passage literally.

RUTH

H   1:1   And it came to pass in the days when the judges judged,
that there was a famine in the land. And a certain man of
Bethlehem in Judah went to sojourn in the field of Moab,
he and his wife, and his two sons.

T   And it came to pass in the days of the leader of leaders[72]
that there was a great famine in the land of Israel. Ten
severe famines were decreed by God[73] to be upon the world,
from the day on which the world was created until the
coming of the King Messiah, by which to chastise those
who dwell on earth. The first famine was in the days of
Adam. The second famine was in the days of Lamech.
The third famine was in the days of Abraham. The fourth
famine was in the days of Isaac. The fifth famine was in
the days of Jacob. The sixth famine was in the days of
Boaz, who was called Ibzan[74] the Righteous of Beth Lehem
of Judah.[75] The seventh famine was in the days of David,
king of Israel. The eighth famine was in the days of Elijah
the Prophet. The ninth famine was in the days of Elisha
in Samaria. The tenth famine is destined to be, not a hunger to eat bread nor a thirst to drink water, but to hear the
word of prophecy from the Lord. And when that famine
was mighty in the land of Israel, a great man went out of
Beth Lehem of Judah and went to dwell in the field of
Moab, he and his wife and his two sons.

MI: רְעָב, "famine," an indirect Messianic derivation.

The Targum has a VR, שְׁפַט, "judge," for the Masoretic שְׁפֹט,
"judging."

The Targumist uses the introductory note of the book for a
Midrashic exposition on the great famines, which, of course, culmi-
nates with the great famine that will precede the Messianic advent,
a hunger for religion. To describe this famine, Amos 8:11 is pre-
sented in virtually a literal Aramaic translation.[76]

RP: The ten famines are enumerated and explained in Genesis
Rabbah 25:3; 40:3 with the only variation that the sixth famine
is said to have occurred in the days when the judges judged, generally, instead of in the days of Boaz-Ibzan specifically, as we have
it here, and one famine which recurs in the world with constant
regularity.

The other versions translate literally.

Ruth

H   3:15   And he said: "Bring the mantle that is upon you and hold
             it." And she held it, and he measured six measures of bar-
             ley, and laid it on her; and he went into the city.

T   And he said: "Take the scarf which is upon you and lay
             hold of it." So she took hold of it. Then he measured out
             six seah of barley and placed them upon her, and the Lord
             gave her strength to carry them. Immediately, it was an-
             nounced through prophecy that the six most righteous men
             of the world were destined to descend from her, each of
             whom would be blessed with six blessings: David, Daniel
             and his companions,[77] and the King Messiah. And Boaz
             went into the city.

There is no definite MI, but the Messianic interpretation is
suggested by the six measures of barley, which was understood
thus in rabbinic thinking.

The idea that each of these would be blessed with six special
blessings also may have been adduced from the six measures of
barley.

This passage reflects the homily of Bar Kappara in Sanhedrin
93a, b: "What of the Scripture, 'He gave me these six barley'[78]
(Ruth 3:17)? What is meant by 'six barley'? If we assume that it
actually means six barley, would it be customary for Boaz to give
six barley as a gift? Rather, it must mean six seah of barley. But
then, would it be customary for a woman to carry six seah? But,
he hinted to her that six sons were destined to descend from her,
each of whom would be blessed with six blessings; and these are
David, the Messiah, Daniel, Hananiah, Mishael, and Azariah."
The Talmud then proceeds to enumerate the six blessings of each,
based on a Scriptural verse pertaining to each. The six blessings
of the Messiah are enumerated in Is. 11:2.

The other versions render this passage literally.

LAMENTATIONS

H   2:22   Thou hast called, as in the day of an appointed feast, my
             terrors on every side, and there was none in the day of the
             Lord's anger that escaped or remained. Those that I have
             dandled and brought up has my enemy destroyed.

T   Mayest Thou proclaim liberty to Thy people of the house
             of Israel by the hand of the King Messiah,[79] just as Thou
             didst by the hand of Moses and Aaron on the day of the
             Passover; so that my young men may gather together all
             around from every place to which they were scattered on
             the day of the mighty wrath of the Lord; there was none
             among them who escaped or remained; my sons whom I
             swathed in linen swaddling clothes and reared in royal com-
             fort, my enemies have destroyed.

MI: כְּיוֹם מוֹעֵד   , "as on the day of an appointed feast," which
the Targumist takes to be the Passover.

מְגוּרֵי is understood as those who live with me, my young men.

The Targum expects the advent of the Messiah to be a re-
enactment of the first drama of Israel's liberation. The Messiah is
expected to be the active agent of deliverance, as were Moses and
Aaron. Usually the comparison is drawn with Moses. The addition
here of Aaron is unusual since there is no priestly Messianic context. If Elijah is supposed to be the High Priest for the Messiah
as Aaron was for Moses, the Targumist does not say so directly.
One might expect this, however, in view of the Targum to 4:22.

There are no RP for this Messianic interpretation.

The other versions are literal.

Lam.

H   4:22   The punishment of your iniquity is accomplished, O daughter of Zion, He will no longer keep you in exile. He will punish your iniquity, O daughter of Edom, He will uncover your sins.

T   After that your sins shall be expiated, O congregation of Zion, and you shall be delivered by the hands of the King Messiah and of Elijah the High Priest, and the Lord will no longer keep you in the Dispersion. At the very same time He will visit upon you your iniquities, O wicked Rome,[80] built up in Italy,[81] and full of armies of the enslaved;[82] Persians shall come and oppress you and capture you for you are exposed before the Lord for your guilt.

The MI in this passage is contextual, not specific.

The expectation that Persia will conquer Rome possibly reflects the historical scene when the Persian Chosroes II defeated the Byzantines and wrested Palestine from them, and marched into Jerusalem 614 C.E., and retained it until 628 C.E.[83]

RP: "For the very day that Menahem (the Comforter i.e., the Messiah) was born, Israel received a full settlement for their sins, for R. Samuel b. R. Nahman said: Israel received a full settlement for their transgressions on the day when the Temple was destroyed,[84] as it is said, 'The punishment of your inquity is accomplished, O daughter of Zion, He will no longer keep you in exile.' (Lam. 4:22)." Numbers Rabbah 13:7.

The other versions translate this verse literally.

ECCLESIASTES

H 1:11 There is no remembrance of the former ones; neither shall there be any remembrance of the latter ones that are to come, among those that shall come after.

T There is no remembrance of former generations, nor shall there be any remembrance of the ones that are to follow among the generations[85] that shall be during the days of the King[86] Messiah.

MI: לְאַחֲרֹנָה , "latter things," understood as the end of time.

This interpretation is probably an allusion to the fact that the wonders of the Messianic age will surpass all others and make them to be forgotten, based on Jer. 23:7 f.[87]

RP: "How many miracles were performed for Israel since they left Egypt and even before Israel left Egypt. Concerning these it is said, 'There is no remembrance of the former things and also of the latter things that are to be.' (Eccl. 1:11). To what then, shall I give remembrance? To the miracles of the World-to-Come."[88] Ecclesiastes Rabbah 1:11.

The other versions are literal translations.

Eccl.

H   7:24   That which is far off, and exceeding deep; who can find it
            out?

T   Behold, all that has happened from the beginning is already
            too remote for mortals to know; and of the day of death
            and of the day when the King Messiah will come who can
            find it out by his wisdom? [89]

MI: עָמֹק, "deep," meaning a deep secret.

Double use of עָמֹק prompts the reflection on the two great un-
knowns, the day of death and the date of the Messianic advent.

This is another instance in which the Targum emphasizes the
futility of trying to ascertain the date of the coming of the Messiah
through calculation or, as is indicated here, through speculation
and reasoning. It is all idle and useless.

There is no RP for the Messianic interpretation of this verse,
but cf. Eccl. R. 11:5.

The other versions render the passage literally.

ESTHER II

H   1:1   Now it came to pass in the days of Ahasuerus—this is Ahasuerus who reigned from India even unto Ethiopia, over a hundred and seven and twenty provinces.

T   And it came to pass in the days of Ahasuerus, he is Ahasuerus, one of the ten kings who ruled or are destined to rule in the world. These are they: The first kingdom is that of the King of Kings, the Lord of hosts, may His kingdom soon be revealed.[90] The second is that of Nimrod. The third is that of Pharoah. The fourth is that of Israel. The fifth is that of Nebuchadnezzar. The sixth is that of Ahasuerus. The seventh is that of Cyrus.[91] The eighth is that of Rome. The ninth is that of the Messiah son of David. The tenth is that of the King of Kings, the Lord of hosts, extolled and exalted be He; whose kingdom will soon be revealed over the inhabitants of the earth.

There is no MI. The Targumist merely takes the occasion to expound his idea of the cycle of history, beginning with God's kingdom and culminating with the final revelation of it. The Messiah is depicted here as the forerunner of the Kingdom of God on earth.

RP: Pirke deR. Eliezer IX, with some variations.

The other versions are literal.

I CHRONICLES

H   3:24   And the sons of Elioenai: Hodaviah, and Eliashib, and Pelaiah, and Akkub, and Johanan, and Delaiah, and Anani, seven.

T   And the sons of Elioenai: Hodaviahu, Eliashib, Pelaiah, Akkub, Johanan, Delaiah, and Anani, who is the King Messiah who is destined to be revealed. Seven in all.

MI: וַעֲנָנִי , "and Anani," which is based on Dan. 7:13, and which here becomes a proper noun, the name of the Messiah. The reference in Daniel reads: וַאֲרוּ עִם עֲנָנֵי שְׁמַיָּא , "And behold, with the clouds of heaven." עֲנָנֵי there is plural in construct with שְׁמַיָּא , and vocalized *anane.* Here it becomes *Anani.*

RP: "If Israel is worthy, עַנֵּי ,[92] (the Messiah will come) with the clouds of heaven." Sanhedrin 98a. But even here it is not a proper noun, but an unusual play on the sound of words, for it continues: "If they are not worthy, עָנִי , 'humble,' and riding on an ass (Zech. 9:9)."

The other versions render this verse literally.

SUMMARY OF THE TARGUM TO THE HAGIOGRAPHA

Messianic interpretations are found in the following passages: Psalms 18:28-32; 21:1-8; 45:1-18; 61:7-9; 72:1-20; 80:15-18; 89:51-52; 132:11-18; Song of Songs 1:8, 17; 4:5; 7:4; 7:12-8:4; Ruth 1:1; 3:15; Lamentations 2:22; 4:22; Ecclesiastes 1:11; 7:24; Esther II 1:1; I Chronicles 3:24.

The Messianic interpretations other than those in Psalms are not too important in the overall picture, because they are peripheral and Midrashic instead of genuinely exegetical. The Messianic rendering in I Chron. 3:24 is of interest in that it demonstrates how an earlier rabbinic homily can be so fixed as to become a proper noun in the course of time.

The Messianic exposition in Psalms adds little in the way of Messianic details, but it does demonstrate once more the tendency on the part of the Targum not to be too liberal in attributing Messianic intentions to the Bible. Psalms 2 and 110, for example, are not rendered Messianically. Of the wealth of Messianic possibilities in the Book of Psalms, the Targum utilizes only a choice few to interpret with reference to the Messiah.

CHAPTER IV

CONCLUSIONS

The detailed study of the Messianic passages in the Targum opens up new vistas of understanding in the area of Messianic exegesis, both Jewish and Christian.

The study also leads to the following conclusions:

1. The official Targumim are quite circumspect about adducing Messianic interpretations from the Hebrew text; when they do they invariably use the simple משיחא for the Messianic designation; the unofficial Targumim are somewhat less cautious, but sparing nevertheless; and whether to the Pentateuch or the Hagiographa, they generally designate the Messiah as מלכא משיחא . We may conjecture that the reason might be that the official Targumim stem from Maccabean times when hope for a restoration of the Davidic kingship would constitute treason to the Hasmonean dynasty.[1] Another possibility is that they were redacted in Babylon, where reference to a royal Jewish Messiah might have been misinterpreted to the detriment of the Jewish populace.

2. While a main current of Messianic thought in general outline is discernible throughout the Targum, individual Messianic interpretations vary in detail, depending upon the nature of the Hebrew text and upon the Targumic mind which fashioned the interpretation in question. There is no absolute consistency or unanimity of viewpoint.

3. In spite of this, it is possible to delineate a portrait of the Messiah as depicted in the Targum, though some of the elements are divergent, and all are not present at all times. According to this picture the Messiah of the Targum has the following features:

The Messiah will be the symbol and/or the active agent of the deliverance of Israel. He will be of Davidic lineage, though he may have a non-Davidic predecessor, the Ephraimite Messiah, who will die in battle. Elijah will herald his coming and will serve as his High Priest. A world conflict will rage between Rome, variously identified with Gog, Amalek, Edom, and Armilus, on the one hand, and Assyria or Eber, on the other, indicating that to the Targumist, Assyria and not Babylon was the real enemy of Israel, and this will result in the annihilation of both at the time of the Messianic advent; the enemies of Israel will be shattered either by divine or Messianic intervention. The Messiah will bring an end to the wandering of Israel, and the Jewish people will be gathered in from their Dispersion to their own land. The Northern Kingdom will be re-united with Judah. The drama of the Exodus from Egypt will be re-enacted; in this drama Moses may participate, made possible by a resurrection of the dead. The Messiah will live eternally. He will restore the Temple and rebuild Jerusalem, which will enjoy divine protection for itself and its inhabitants. He will have sovereignty over all the world and make the Torah the universal law of mankind, with the ideal of education being realized to the full. The Messiah will have the gift of prophecy, and may have intercessory power to seek forgiveness of sin, but he will punish the unrepenting wicked of his people, as well as of the nations, and have the power to cast them into Gehenna. There will be a moral regeneration of Israel and of mankind. The Messiah will be a righteous judge, dispensing justice and equity, the champion of the poor and the oppressed, the personification of social justice. He will reward the righteous, who will surround him and eternally enjoy the divine effulgence. The essence of the Messiah will be faith in God; and he will vindicate that faith, and the faithfulness of Israel, in the eyes of all the world.

4. Targumic Messianism, for the most part, is a reflection of rabbinic Messianism, which was the environment in which it flourished; but in its Messianic exegesis the Targum displays remarkable independence, at times offering Messianic interpretations which have no parallel whatsoever in other rabbinic sources. It is a living, dynamic, challenging exegetical force.

5. There is little evidence, if any, of any direct dependence of the Targum on LXX, but there are some areas in which both versions understand the text Messianically. On the other hand, there is

ample evidence that in certain passages the Vulgate leans heavily on the Messianic interpretations of the Targum. The Syriac parallels the Targum occasionally. The Arabic is quite late, and generally echoes one or another of the earlier versions. The influence of the Targum on Christian exegesis has been clearly demonstrated in the course of this study. Pertinent passages are: Gen. 3:15; Num. 23:21 and 24:24; Is. 16:1 and the Servant passages of Deutero-Isaiah, 42:1 ff. and 52:13 ff.; Hosea 14:8; and Micah 4:8.

6. Our critical analysis has disclosed that there was a remarkably faithful transmission of Messianic material in the text of the Targum, notwithstanding the length of time and the many hands through which it passed, and in spite of textual corruptions due to scribal and typographical inaccuracies, Messianic glosses were not interpolated where one might expect to find them, as in Ezekiel, nor were Messianic interpretations deleted where they appeared to be out of harmony with the mainstream of Jewish Messianic exegesis, as in Psalm 80:16.

7. Incidental to our main theme, but relevant to it nevertheless, we have structured Messianism within the framework of Jewish history. It is our contention that the architects of Jewish Messianism are the prophet Isaiah and his disciples, and that the historical event which precipitated it was the Assyrian crisis. Psychologically, Messianism contains a survivalistic ego-structure which reverts to the Assyrian crisis. The Targum tends to support this contention in its sensitive rendering of the Messianic passages in Isaiah.

8. Also incidental to our main theme, but relevant to it, is the discovery through some Targumic Messianic interpretations, that the previously accepted *terminus ad quem* of Targum Jonathan to the Prophets, placing it at a point in history prior to the Arab conquest of Babylon, is erroneous, and that it must be placed at some date subsequent to the Arab conquest, possibly even with Saadia Gaon. This contention, first projected in this study, is elaborated by the author elsewhere.[2]

LITERAL TRANSLATIONS OF HEBREW
MASHIAH, "ANOINTED"

Mention must be made of the Targumic method of rendering literally by its Aramaic equivalent, those passages of Scripture where the Hebrew term מׁשׁיח is used, as "anointed one." These passages are not Messianic as defined and understood in this analytical study, and may apply to any one chosen by God to be a king, and anointed as such. Because these passages are rendered by forms of the Aramaic word מׁשׁיחא, "anointed one," and because there is a possibility of their being misunderstood as Messianic, we list them here: I Samuel 2:35;[1] 12:3, 5; 16:6; 24:7, 11; 26:9, 11, 16, 23; II Samuel 1:14, 16; 22:51;[2] Isaiah 45:1;[3] Habakkuk 3:13;[4] Psalms 2:2;[5] 18:51;[6] 20:7; 28:8; 84:10; 89:29; 132:10;[7] II Chronicles 6:42.

INTRODUCTION

NOTES

1. Foremost exponent of this view is Hugo Gressmann, *Der Messias* (Goettingen: Vandenhoeck und Ruprecht, 1929), p. 231 f., and elsewhere; "The Sources of Israel's Messianic Hope," *American Journal of Theology*, XVII, 1913, pp. 176 ff. Also W. O. E. Oesterley, *The Evolution of the Messianic Idea* (New York: Dutton, 1909), cited by J. Sarachek, *The Doctrine of the Messiah in Medieval Jewish Literature* (New York: Jewish Theological Seminary, 1932), p. 3; and others.

2. J. H. Greenstone, *The Messiah Idea in Jewish History* (Philadelphia: Jewish Publication Society, 1906), p. 21; J. Klausner, *Ha-Ra'yon Ha-Meshihi B'yisrael* (Tel-Aviv: Masadah, 5710), pp. 10 ff. and pp. 318 f.; *American Journal of Theology*, XIV, 1910, pp. 337 ff.; Sarachek, *loc. cit.*

3. George F. Moore, *Judaism* (Cambridge: Harvard University Press, 1927), I, 291 ff. An excellent survey of the entire development of the doctrine of the Messiah, though open to dispute on some points, is given by C. W. Emmet, "Messiah," *Hastings Encyclopaedia of Religion and Ethics.*

4. Klausner, *op. cit.*, p. 31.

5. J. Bowker, *The Targums and Rabbinic Literature* (Cambridge University Press, 1969), which has several selections from the Targumim to Genesis which touch on the Messianic theme analytically. J. F. Stenning, *The Targum of Isaiah* (Oxford, 1949), *ad loc. Christology of the Targums* (Edinburgh, Robert Young, n. d.), is a haphazard collection of passages in poor English translation and without any comment whatsoever, critical or otherwise.

6. Emmet takes Christian interpreters to task for this failing, *loc. cit.* Jewish scholars are no exceptions. Greenstone, *op. cit.* and Sarachek, *op. cit.*, are very negligent in this respect. Cf. also the idea of Reform Judaism, of a Messianic Age without a Messiah.

7. See Moore, *op. cit.*, II, 279-395; especially his observation, p. 346.

8. Roughly from the second century B.C.E. to the ninth century C.E. See S. H. Levey, "The Date of Targum Jonathan to the Prophets," *Vetus Testamentum,* XXI, No. 2, 1971, pp. 186 ff.

9. Inasmuch as this, too, is considered a vindication of the righteous at the culmination of history.

10. Ezek. 17:22-24; 34:23-24; 37:21-28. Another exception is the

Targum to Amos 9:11. On the problem of the Targum to Ezekiel, see *infra*, pp. 78-87.

11. On rabbinic eschatology and Messianism, see Moore, *loc. cit.;* Greenstone, *op. cit.,* Chapters II and III; K. Kohler, "Eschatology," and M. Buttenwieser, "Messiah," in *The Jewish Encyclopedia.*

12. A. Sperber, *The Bible in Aramaic,* Leiden, Brill, 1959; 1962; 1968.

13. A. Berliner, *Targum Onkelos* (Berlin: Gorzelanczyk and Co., 1884).

14. P. de Lagarde, *Prophetae Chaldaice* (Leipzig: Teubneri, 1872); and *Hagiographa Chaldaice* (Leipzig: Teubneri, 1873).

15. M. Ginsburger, *Das Fragmententhargum* (Berlin: S. Calvary and Co., 1899); and *Pseudo-Jonathan* (Berlin: S. Calvary and Co., 1903).

16. A. Diez Macho, *Neophyti I,* 2 vols. Targum Palestinense Ms de la Biblioteca Vaticana, Madrid-Barcelona, 1970.

17. *Mikraoth Gedoloth,* [Biblia Rabbinica] (Pieterkov: P. Belchatovsky, 1888); and *Mikraoth Gedoloth* (New York: Pardes Publishing House, 1951), a photographic reprint of the original Warsaw edition.

CHAPTER I

NOTES

1. Or, "aim," יכוין. This depicts the concept of כונה as a moral force. N has a confusion of person, reading "you will aim and wound him," etc.

2. "The Holy One, blessed be He, said to Israel: My sons, I have created the evil impulse, but I have also created the Torah as its antidote, and if you engage in Torah you will not be committed into its hand." Kiddushin 30b and elsewhere.

3. Charles A. Briggs, *Messianic Prophecy* (New York: Charles Scribner's Sons, 1886), pp. 71 ff.; J. Skinner, *A Critical and Exegetical Commentary on Genesis* (New York: Charles Scribner's Sons, 1910), p. 81, traces this to Irenaeus.

4. The entire second half is missing in N. It would seem to me that *Neophyti I* is a combination of PsJ and F.

5. קץ, *"Ketz,"* a technical term used in Messianic speculation.

6. Literally, "tribes."

7. קץ, *"Ketz."*

8. P reads: "When the glory of the Shekinah of the Lord was revealed to him, the date of the end when the King Messiah would arrive was concealed from him." The rendering of G implies that the revelation of the date came in a flash and vanished immediately. N omits the Messianic reference.

9. Use of the simple term משיחא "Messiah," rather than מלכא משיחא "King Messiah" stamps this as being intimately bound up with the official Targumim, which never use anything but the simple term משיחא to designate the Messiah.

10. P has F in closer parallel with PsJ but without any Messianic reference.

11. A. H. Silver, *Messianic Speculation in Israel* (New York: The Macmillan Company, 1927), pp. 13 ff.

12. Strictly speaking, there was some doubt if Bar Kokhba could have been the Messiah since there was some doubt about his Davidic lineage, and it is puzzling that R. Akiba would regard him as such except in desperation. Cf. Klausner, *op. cit.,* p. 231, and Moore, *op. cit.,* II, 329.

13. Klausner, *op. cit.,* pp. 248 ff.; Moore, *op. cit.,* II, pp. 345 f. and 352 f.

14. Pesahim 54b.

15. Sanhedrin 97b.

16. Derek Eretz Rabbah, XI.

17. It is a strange coincidence that this ritual interpretation should issue from two descendants of Temple functionaries.

18. According to SP. B reads, "He who exercises dominion."

19. I have here used SP's version, מֵילָא מֵילָא , in preference to B who reads, מֵילָא מֵילָא , which would have the meaning "and his garment, individually, (literally, one matter at a time), of the finest bright dye," and which is awkward in construction. M. Jastrow, *A Dictionary of the Targumim* (London, 1903), II, p. 773, sub מֵילָא I also regards this reading as preferable. P concurs.

20. SP. B reads, "hills."

21. The perpetuation of the scribe-educator in the descendants of Judah is probably designed to fill the historical gap between the end of the political rule of the Davidic line and the advent of the Messiah in the remote future, the Messiah becoming a combination of the two—a king-educator. Cf. Is. 30:20, which J, however, takes as referring to God and not the Messiah.

22. Reads שָׁלַח for שִׁילֹה .

23. A play on the similarity of the names, thus rendering honor to their teacher. The Talmud continues that the school of R. Jannai claimed the Messiah's name was Jinnon, and the school of R. Hananiah said it was Hananiah, each quoting an appropriate proof-text.

24. Literally, "grapes." An ellipsis, with the obvious meaning "like those of the presser of grapes, which are saturated with wine."

25. P continues here with "therefore his mountains and his wine cellars shall be red with wine, and his hills shall be white with harvest and with sheepfolds." G regards this addition as another version entirely.

26. Psychologically, the vengeance is probably a retaliation in kind.

27. See Moore, *op. cit.*, I, 466 f.

28. In the version of P.

29. The entire tone is apocalyptic. Cf. Rev. 19:11-15, which is striking in its resemblance to this passage.

30. See Samuel Krauss, "Jerome," *The Jewish Encyclopedia;* and G. Grutzmacher, "Jerome," *Hasting's Encyclopaedia of Religion and Ethics.*

31. P: "scholars."

32. P reads "kings and rulers are slain."

33. Literally, "with."

34. P: "rivers."

35. G reads מזוננין , "clear," which makes no sense.

36. G omits the last phrase, as well as v. 12.

37. H. Graetz, *History of the Jews* (Philadelphia: Jewish Publication Society, 1893), II, 421 ff.

38. The text is corrupt, and reads "right hand" here also. G omits this entire verse completely. The rendering "hand" is on the basis of PsJ, *ad loc.*, but where there is no Messianic reference.

39. *"Ketz."*

40. The parallel is even more striking when we consider the Targumic word for "lead," יְדַבֵּר which might have been taken in its Hebrew meaning Also, Mark 9:9, "This is my beloved son."

41. Note the use of the simple form, מְשִׁיחָא, rather than "King Messiah." N like F omits the Messianic reference.

42. N has no Messianic reference here, just as F has none, reinforcing my contention that N is not a thoroughgoing manuscript of PsJ, but a confusion of PsJ and F.

43. PsJ to Exod. 6:18b: "And the years of the life of Kehat, the pious, were one hundred thirty-three. He lived to see Phineas, who is Elijah the High Priest, who will be sent to the Dispersion of Israel at the end of days." The same thought is expressed in Baba Bathra 121b. Cf. Moore, *op. cit., II,* 359 ff. and Klausner, *op. cit.,* pp. 268 ff.

44. Mekilta to Exod. 16:33.

45. Justin Martyr, *Dialogue with Trypho,* 8:4 and 49:1, Vol. VI of *Fathers of the Church,* trans. T. B. Falls (New York: Christian Heritage Press, 1949).

46. Moore, *op. cit.,* II, 370 ff., discusses this problem, terms the Ephraimite Messiah idea "a curious aberration." A more detailed discussion of the problem of the Messiah son of Joseph (another appellation of the Messiah son of Ephraim) is found in Klausner, *op. cit.,* pp. 289-301.

47. The word used is not the usual יְיָ (יהוה), but קִירִיס, the Greek, *Kúrios,* perhaps a veiled Messianic hint.

48. Cf. Sib. Or., 3:97 ff.

49. Sanhedrin 52a and Yalkut Shimeoni to Lev. 10:1, 2.

50. Genesis Rabbah 56:9. Yalkut Shimeoni to Zech. 9:14.

51. Yalkut Shimeoni, *loc. cit.,* quoting Sifre, Behalothecha. On the eschatological nature of the Messianic trumpet, Klausner, *op. cit.,* p. 281.

52. Yalkut Shimeoni to Is. 27:13.

53. Literally, "and the Messiah shall be anointed out of Israel."

54. Moore, *op. cit.,* II, 115, 116, 371.

55. Moore, *op. cit.,* I, 89; II, 329, 349.

56. Note the use of the simple form, מְשִׁיחָא.

57. Either a censorial substitution for Rome, or a reflection of later history. The passage "from Constantinople" to "Caesarea," stricken by censor in G.

58. So G, צִיעָן. P reads צִיצִין, "wings of an army."

59. Omitted in P.

60. P adds "and destroy."

61. Note the different interpretation of עֹשֶׂה חָיִל, from O and PsJ. P renders 18a thus: "Persia shall inherit Mt. Gabla from their enemies," etc.

62. The last phrase is omitted in P.

63. P renders v. 23 thus: "Woe unto him who is alive when the Memra of the Lord gets set to reward the righteous and punish the wicked."

64. G reads בערברבניא , "with mixed multitudes," instead of בלברניא .

65. P reads: "from the great empire."

66. It does not stand to reason that a Jewish interpretation such as LXX would expect affliction or destruction of the Jews in the Messianic age; however a Christian interpretation such as V would find it in keeping with its theology. There is some possibility that LXX shows signs of Christian redaction at this point.

67. PsJ to Exod. 17:16. Also to Num. 24:20.

68. One who took this injunction seriously was the great scholar M. Jastrow, who omitted the word and a discussion of it from his *Dictionary of the Targumim*. It is difficult to conceive of this as a mere oversight. Also, J. Levy, *Chaldäisches Wörterbuch über die Targumim*.

69.   יצרא בישא, Aramaic equivalent of the Hebrew יצר הרע .

70.   יצרא טבא, Aramaic equivalent of the Hebrew יצר טוב .

71. For a discussion of the evil impulse, see Moore, *op. cit.*, I, 479 ff. Cf. also H. Hirschberg, "Eighteen Hundred Years Before Freud," *Judaism*, X (1961) pp. 129-141.

72. Sukkah 52a.

73. Moore, *op. cit.*, I, 48 3ff Genesis Rabbah 14:4. But cf. ARN, 16, where good impulse emerges at age 13.

CHAPTER II

NOTES

1. So L and W. Omitted in SP.

2. קל , "noise," "sound," or "voice."

3. W reads "Magog."

4. *Supra,* p. 19.

5. Or, "according to My Memra."

6. משיחי , which can be rendered either "My anointed" or "My Messiah."

7. Briggs, *op. cit.,* pp. 126 ff.

8. There is an undetected typographical error in SP 7:12 וחשכוב for ותשכוב .

9. So L, כבר. W is even more explicit: דמי כבר , "likened unto a son," or, more accurately, "resembling a son." SP, לבר, follows the Hebrew precisely.

10. S. H. Hooke, *Judaism and Christianity,* ed. W. O. E. Oesterley (New York: The Macmillan Company, 1937), I, 240. In connection with the Jewish interpretation of the Servant passages in Isaiah, he says: "The date of the fixing of the Targum tradition is too early to allow of an explanation of this phenomenon as the result of Christian influence, that is, as an attempt to refute the early Christian use of the passage as a prophecy of the death and resurrection of the Messiah."

J. Bowker, *The Targums and Rabbinic Literature* (Cambridge, University Press, 1969, p. xi) on the other hand, makes this generalization: "They [The Targums] are, therefore indispensable for Jewish thought in that period; they are equally important for the study of the Patristic period of the Church, since they frequently represent the other side of the Christian-Jewish debate. Christians tended to base their arguments against Judaism on verses of scripture, and the Targum–interpretation of those verses was often deliberately designed to exclude the Christian argument."

The author, on the basis of his own study, agrees with Bowker, in the main, but thinks he is too dogmatically certain and too general in his assertion.

Prof. Willis W. Fisher in a discussion with the author, suggests that the Targum's exegetical method in this passage, and similarly elsewhere, may provide the clue to Ezekiel 1 and other passages where "like," "resembling," "having the appearance of," etc. are used to introduce imagery that may otherwise have been construed anthropomorphically. This may point to a very late redaction of Ezekiel, incorporating Targumic-rabbinic methodology.

11. SP: "in His Memra."

12. S. H. Levey, "The Date of Targum Jonathan to the Prophets," *Vetus Testamentum,* Vol. XXI, No. 2, April 1971, pp. 186 ff.

13. This wording is that of Saadia Gaon: ليس إلا• غير الرب *A* to Ps. 18:32, is more idiomatic and goes back to the exact wording of the Moslem article of faith. Cf. S. H. Levey, "The Date of Targum Jonathan to the Prophets," *Vetus Testamentum,* Vol. XXI, No. 2, April 1971, pp. 186 ff.

14. So SP, which is closer to the original Hebrew than L, who reads בסיס , "footstool," "stand," "base," probably a scribal or typographical error.

15. Literally, "and he said," or "thought."

16. So SP. W reads "his glory."

17. The Seven Days of Creation. Cf. V's rendering of Zechariah 3:8, "*Oriens.*" *Infra,* p. 97.

18. Literally, "as the arrangement of creation."

19. Tanhuma to Sidra Bereshith, 6. Also J to Judges 5:31.

20. Genesis Rabbah 3:6 and Exodus Rabbah 15:21.

21. 4:33 in the other versions.

22. So SP and L. W reads: "and in the Messianic World-to-Come."

23. *Infra,* p. 115.

24. Kimhi, *ad loc.,* gives us a variant Targumic reading found in neither SP nor W, ועבדי ארעא , "and those who till the soil," closer to the idea of the Hebrew text, though not as close to the Targumic context.

25. Or, "decisive."

26. L adds "of glory."

27. M. Peah 1:1.

28. Based on Jer. 23:5, and Zech. 3:8 and 6:12, and elsewhere. "R. Joshua b. Levi said: His (Messiah's) name is צמח," Lamentations Rabbah 1:51. For the appropriation and use of the term as a Messianic name, see Moore, *op. cit.,* II, 325, and Klausner, *op. cit.,* pp. 60 ff. and 112 ff.

29. In the versions, 9:6 ff.

30. Or, "to observe it."

31. Literally, "and his name has been called from before the One who gives," etc. I have deliberately adhered to the Targumic sentence structure, which beyond question makes the appellations of deity the subject, and Messiah the object.

32. Or "merit."

33. R. Hillel: "Israel will have no Messiah, since they have already consumed him (his coming was consummated) in the days of Hezekiah," San-

hedrin 98b-99a. R. Johanan b. Zakkai: "Prepare a throne for Hezekiah king of Judah, who is coming," Berakot 28b. Also Bar Kappara in Lamentations Rabbah on 1:16. Johanan's statement is especially significant, for it was he who salvaged what little he could in 70 C.E.

34. Sanhedrin 94b.

35. Thus Bar Kappara, Sanhedrin 94a. The proof lies in this, that the closed *mem* represents the closing or end of Hezekiah's prospects of being the Messiah.

36. So SP. W: "bring down upon." L: "call down upon."

37. So L. SP: "his scourge."

38. According to L. SP: "a spirit from before the Lord."

39. Or "to the fear of Him."

40. SP cites the Codex Reuchlinianus as adding here: "This Messiah who is destined to come will teach the law, and will judge in the fear of the Lord."

41. L adds "of the land."

42. So L and W. L reads אדמלנן , corrected to ארמלנוס , but both are variants. Armilus, a disguised form of Romulus, for Rome, is found in the late apocalypses and is a Messianic legend mentioned by Saadia Gaon, representing the anti-Messiah. Jastrow, *op. cit.,* p. 123, sub ארמילוס . Sarachek, *op. cit.,* p. 43. Ginzberg, "Armilus," *Jewish Encyclopedia.*

43. Literally, "the son's son."

44. Or "household," "family."

45. Literally, "in which they can walk in sandals."

46. Ginzberg, *loc. cit.*

47. Genesis Rabbah 98:9. Cf. Rom. 15:12, also quoting this verse.

48. Lamentations Rabbah 1:51. This story and its variant versions are discussed by Gressmann, *Der Messias,* pp. 449 ff.

49. So W, which follows the Hebrew, reading כחיוי מפריח , which is also the version quoted by Kimhi, *ad loc.* SP and L read מפרית, with a variant מפריד, both of which would mean "the dismembering serpent," i.e., the basilisk, whose look was believed to cause a person's limbs to fall apart.

50. So SP. L: "I will slay your mighty ones"; W: "but he shall slay your sons."

51. Kimhi, *ad loc.*

52. I.e., in the sense of being under the Messiah's dominion.

53. So L. SP reads: "because the mountain of the Congregation of Zion has been like a desert," Kimhi's version: "the Messiah of Israel, who will become mighty, because they were in the desert," etc.

54. Reference is to Moab.

55. So L. Omitted in SP.

56. So L. SP reads: "Make your shade like the night, like the daylight in the midst of a bright sky."

57. So W. SP and L read: "Vanished are those who used to thresh the earth." Presumably in a destructive manner, such as with salt.

58. Genesis Rabbah, Soncino, NV 97, p. 907 f.

59. Rashi, Kimhi, Metzudat Zion, *ad loc.*

60. George B. Gray, *A Critical and Exegetical Commentary on the Book of Isaiah* (New York: Charles Scribner's Sons, 1912), p. 289.

61. So L, W, and others. Omitted in SP.

62. In Is. 44:1 and 45:4 the identification is made explicitly in the Hebrew text.

63. It is interesting that Rashi, who, because of the troubled period of the Crusades during which he lived, frequently interpreted Messianically, interprets this passage exactly as does LXX. Kimhi, however, takes it as Messianic.

64. The verb "to be" is implied. Otherwise, the expression "My servant the Messiah" would refer back to "You," meaning Israel, as Messiah. This would be inconsistent with Targumic Messianic interpretation.

65. L reads: "that I am the Lord."

66. So L and W. SP reads: "the righteous ones."

67. תולדת , literally, "that which springs from," or "results."

68. The expression קודשא, referring to person, applies to God, especially when qualified, but in this instance it seems to apply to the Messiah.

69. So SP and W. The reading of L, אוולא , "first," makes no sense, unless it is a Christological insertion referring to the second coming of Christ, the surreptitious work of a Christian scribe.

70. Or, "shall gaze at him." יסתכל has both meanings. Our preference is based on the context, associated with the preceding phrase.

71. Or, "rehearse," according to SP and L.

72. The exact meaning is not clear. Possibly this refers to retribution, a prelude to v. 9.

73. So L and W. SP reads: "One shall not speak of material possessions with their mouth."

74. So SP. L reads "the wicked," which is possible if we assume that the Targumist has purgatory in mind. In v. 9, the wicked Jews were committed to Gehenna, and perhaps here they have already served their sentence, and are ready for better things.

75. L has a typographical error here, שעבור for שעבוד .

76. Kimhi reads here, "from the palace."

77. Literally, "under the subjugation of."

78. Churgin, *op. cit.,* p. 26.

79. *Supra,* pp. 9-10. .

80. Yalkut Shimeoni to Is. 52:13.

81. Or "dismayed."

82. J seems impelled to explain the name יְהֹוָה צִדְקֵנוּ paraphrastically and in full, probably because the kernel of the Messianic idea is found in it.

83. יְהֹוָה . This does not mean that the author of this quotation believes God to be the King Messiah, but merely that he thinks this will be the Messiah's appellation. Compare Christian usage with reference to Jesus.

84. W reads "the Chaldeans," thus making it apply to the Babylonian Exile directly. This also applies to "nations" in 30:8b.

85. W reads, "your."

86. The proof lies, according to the author of this statement in the Talmud, in the Biblical use of the imperfect rather than the perfect tense.

87. Literally, "give them to."

88. See note 82 on Jer. 23:6, *supra*.

89. Literally, "to perform the slaughter of the sacred things."

90. J uses the word יניק to denote "child," a clever exegetical device relating to the Hebrew יְנִקוֹתָיו -"his branches."

91. Literally, "kingdom."

92. L and W read "on."

93. Kimhi reads "great."

94. L at this point reads: גזרית , "I have decreed," which is probably scribal dittography from the end of the verse.

95. Literally, "with arm." The rhythmic rhyme of the Aramaic is interesting דִּבְרֹשַׁע וּבִדְרָע .

96. L: "nations."

97. The word פרנס, as verb and as noun, in the twofold sense of "to lead" and "to provide for."

98. L:רבא, "chief," "master," with מלכא ,"king," as a marginal note.

99. SP reads ואזגר , probably a scribal or typographical error.

100. Literally, "established" or "permanent."

101. Literally, "the recipients of humiliation."

102. W adds: "against Me."

103. Briggs, *op. cit.*, p. 270 f.

104. II Kings 25:18; Jer. 52:24.

105. I.e., the crown.

106. The expression is based on the triple use of עוה, in the Hebrew text, which the Targumist interprets as sin.

107. Gedaliah.

108. II Kings 25:25; Jer. 41:1 ff.

109. Berliner, *op. cit.*, pp. 108 ff., theorizes that all the Targumim were suppressed in Palestine, but he does not prove the point, and his view is not widely accepted.

110. Churgin, *op. cit.*, Chap. I. Also W. Bacher, "Targum" in *The Jewish Encyclopedia.*

111. E. g., under Hadrian, 135-138 C.E.

112. Such as R. Akiba and his contemporaries.

113. Or "of many noises."

114. Commenting on Hos. 3:5, the Rabbis argue: "This refers to the King Messiah. If he comes from the living, his name will be David, and if from those that sleep, his name will be David." J. Berakot 5a. This may have been a subterfuge to confuse the Romans to whom Messianism was treason.

115. Sanhedrin 99a. Rashi *ad loc.,* correctly interprets this as implying that R. Hillel expected divine, not human, deliverance, i.e., eschatologically, not Messianically.

116. What is true of the Targum to Ezekiel is also true of the Targum to Amos, which renders Amos 9:11 thus: "At that time I will reestablish the fallen kingdom of David, and will rebuild their cities and repair their synagogues; and it (the Davidic dynasty) shall rule over every kingdom, and shall put an end to and destroy great armies, and it shall be rebuilt and firmly established on its foundations as in days of old."

117. 1:11 in the English versions.

118. Literally, "give."

119. 14:4 in English versions.

120. Literally, "tree."

121. Literally, "shoots."

122. Literally, "memorial."

123. Literally, "old wine."

124. Leviticus Rabbah 1:2. Numbers Rabbah 8:1.

125. *Supra,* p. 7.

126. See the Targum on Micah 5:1, which follows. For a thorough discussion of the entire problem, see Moore, *op. cit.* II, 343 ff.

127. Verse 2 in the versions.

128. Literally, "from the days of the world."

129. L reads: "in." Rashi, in Sanhedrin 98b, supports the version of SP and W used here.

130. This verse, which is quite obscure in the Hebrew, is explained somewhat more clearly in the Targum, but remains obscure.

131. The Targumist felt awkward about attributing the might of God even to the Messiah, and hence translates, lit., "with a might from before the Lord."

132. Moore, *op. cit.,* II, 343 f. But cf. Pesikta Rabbati 33:6.

133. The name of the Messiah, together with the Torah, repentance, Paradise, Hell, God's throne, and the Temple, was created before the world

was brought into being. Pesahim 54a.

134. Moore, *op. cit.*, II, 361.

135. Sanhedrin 98b, and Rashi to Mic. 5:2.

136. W reads עובדי כוכבים, ומזלות , "pagans."

137. קיסומא , literally "rakings."

138. Compare the Targumic introduction to II Sam. 22:32, *supra*, pp. 38-39 and to Ps. 18:32, *infra*, p. 106.

139. Churgin, *op. cit.*, pp. 22 f. While Churgin discusses Hab. 3:17 he completely disregards v. 18 and its implications.

140. For a discussion of this situation, see H. Graetz, *History of the Jews* (Philadelphia: Jewish Publication Society, 1893), II, 129 ff.

141. L has here "Hananiah, Mishael, and Azariah"; the Talmud, Sanhedrin 93a, takes this part of the verse as referring to these three.

142. L adds: "of Rome."

143. Moore, *op. cit.*, II, 325.

144. L: "he shall take up arms," reading זין rather than זיו

145. L omits "high."

146. So L and W, following the Biblical text. SP has "a peaceful kingdom," vocalizing מָלְכָא instead of מלכא.

147. See discussion in connection with the Servant passages of Deutero-Isaiah, *supra*, pp. 63 ff.

148. See *supra*, p. 36.

CHAPTER III

NOTES

1. The Talmud, Shabbat 115a, mentions a ban placed on the Targum to Job by Gamaliel I (first half of first century C.E., the Gamaliel of Acts 5:34 ff.), and it is assumed that the Targum to Job and the Targum to Psalms had a common origin. (W. Bacher, "Targum," in *The Jewish Encyclopedia.*)

2. The author has demonstrated that the Targum to Ruth probably contains a reference to the prohibition of polygamy by R. Gershon of Mayence (960-1040), which would place this reference in the eleventh century C. E. S. H. Levey, "The Targum to the Book of Ruth: Its Linguistic and Exegetical Character" (Unpublished thesis, Hebrew Union College, 1934), pp. 2 f.

3. Briggs, *op. cit.,* pp. 134 ff. Some rabbinic sources likewise: Exodus Rabbah 1:1 understands this as a reference to the Wars of Gog and Magog, as does Berakot 10a.

4. Reference to the purity and innocence of the newly-born child. Compare this passage with the Targum to II Sam. 7:14, *supra,* p. 37.

5. In the other versions this is v. 27. Throughout the Psalms the chapter and verse divisions vary with the versions. In this study, the number of chapter and verse follows the Hebrew.

6. Literally, "reduced to poverty," "unfortunate."

7. Literally, "which is dripping."

8. For the Targumic exegesis, *supra,* pp. 38-39.

9. *Supra,* p. 39 and note 12, II.

10. Or, "sing."

11. This is the usual Targumic rendering of the Hebrew סֶלָה .

12. Baba Bathra 123b; Sukkah 52a.

13. Sukkah 52a.

14. Cf. Moore, *op. cit.,* II, 370 f.

15. Literally, "The tongue of my brain speaks."

16. L adds, "to slay kings and rulers."

17. Literally, "on the matter of."

18. L adds, "to slay armies."

19. Literally, "the sons of your bows," i.e. "arrows."

20. The exact identity of this country is in doubt. The Targumist builds on the Hebrew מִנִּי . Minyas has been suggested. The Aramaic מארע מני also suggests Armenia. Jastrow, *op. cit.,* sub מני .

21. Even as an imaginative projection of the Messianic scroll of the Torah, this would be a supreme work of scribal art. It might not, however, conform to the Halakah, which requires black, vegetable ink. (Soferim 1:1).

22. It is for this reason that we have preferred the version of W to that of L, as being more in keeping with the Messianic portrait; although v. 6 retains the figure of the arrows.

23. Briggs, *op. cit.,* pp. 140 ff.

24. Verse 6 in the English versions.

25. Omitted in W.

26. Literally, "halakot," referring to the Halakah.

27. The construction and meaning are not entirely clear, just as they aren't in the Hebrew.

28. Literally, "in the presence of the shining of the moon."

29. ימא רבא , "the great sea," usually applied to the Mediterranean.

30. ימא דאוקינוס , "the Sea of Oceanus," probably the Mediterranean, possibly the Atlantic.

31. T follows the Hebrew, which refers back to "the poor" in v. 12.

32. Ambiguous, as in the Hebrew. Probably refers to humans.

33. *Supra,* p. 92 and note 133, II.

34. Sanhedrin 98b.

35. Verse 14 in the other versions.

36. L has an uncorrected error here, יסתכר for יסתכל, which W reads, and which we have used.

37. Note the literal rendering of this anthropomorphism. It is characteristic of the later Targumim that they find no problem in anthropomorphism, and make no attempt to soften or reinterpret such expressions.

38. The vine, i.e., Israel, reference to vv. 9 and 15.

39. בר נש -the usual Aramaic expression denoting "man" or "human being." But the reference in a Messianic context is noteworthy.

40. See *supra,* pp. 85 ff.

41. Briggs, *op. cit.,* pp. 132 ff.

42. Of the Temple, when he built and dedicated it. Refers back to v. 8.

43. For the list of references where the Targum merely translates the Hebrew משיח by its Aramaic equivalent משיחא, but without Messianic connotation, see *infra,* Appendix, p. 145.

44. So L. SP reads: "It is incumbent upon you to see the Dispersion . . . the congregation of Israel . . . will be contrite, and He will love her when she walks," etc.

45. Or "order."

46. So SP. L reads: "shall build for them."

47. This reference provides not only a clue as to the date of authorship of this Targum but to conditions under Moslem rule as well.

48. Song of Songs Rabbah 4:5.
49. Rome.
50. So SP. L and W read: "the merit of the righteous who are filled with the commandments like the pomegranate (is filled with seeds)."
51. "The *Ketz.*"
52. SP reads plural.
53. L and W read the passive, יתאמר.
54. SP is corrupt.
55. L and W: "balsam."
56. L and W: "generations."
57. Literally, "scribal."
58. SP reads דנאת, "which has been lying dormant for you."
59. A play on words: the same word also means "tastes."
60. SP reads "Thy Godhead."
61. "Messiah" is omitted in SP.
62. Note the demonology, and the magical significance which the mezuzah has by this time assumed. Cf. A.Z. 11a; Gen. R. 35:3.
63. Omitted in SP.
64. SP reads instead: "that they should leave Jerusalem."
65. Song of Songs Rabbah 1:1. It was probably this interpretation that saved this book for the canon. M. Yadaim, 3:5.
66. In the Targum there are all sorts of participants in the discourse, such as Solomon, the angel Michael, depicted as a teacher of Israel, the ministering angels, etc., etc.
67. Enoch 60:7 ff.; 4 Esdras 6:51 f.
68. Moore, *op. cit.,* II, 363 ff. has an excellent and detailed discussion of this theme.
69. Sanhedrin 99a.
70. There may be some remote connection with the legend that the pomegranate sprang from the blood of Dionysus, but we have been unable to trace it beyond this mere suggestion.
71. Song of Songs Rabbah 4:12.
72. Or, "leader par excellence," whom the Targumist identifies as Ibzan, another name for Boaz.
73. Literally, "Heaven," a metonymy for God.
74. W reads Abzan.
75. Judges 12:8-10.
76. The Targum to Ruth did not copy J to Amos. Its language is entirely different.
77. Hananiah, Mishael, and Azariah, Dan. 1:6 ff.
78. The Hebrew text does not contain any reference to measure.
79. L omits "King." The absence of the appellation "King," which dominates T to the Hagiographa, could conceivably point to a J authorship

since Lamentations is associated with Jeremiah. The version of SP is preferable. But note "King Messiah" in T 4:22, *infra*.

80. So L. W reads, "O daughter of Edom." SP omits the reference to the King Messiah, and Elijah, and the Persians.

81. "Italy" is omitted in W.

82. Or, "hordes of the enslaved."

83. M. Abel, *Histoire de la Palestine,* Paris 1952, II, pp. 388 ff. Cf. also, A. Rhine article, "Chosroes II," *JE* IV, 46.

84. This is associated with a tradition that the Messiah was born at the very time that the Temple was destroyed, and was carried off by a whirlwind. Lamentations Rabbah 1:57. In the same discussion, it is suggested that the name of the Messiah is "Comforter," since the Hebrew word for "Comforter," מנחם, has the same numerical value as צמח, "branch," which is 138. Compare the idea of a Comforter with the Paraclete in John 14:15 ff.

85. SP reads "generation."

86. SP omits "King." See note 79 *supra*.

87. *Supra*, p. 69.

88. In rabbinic sources often confused and identified with the age of the Messiah.

89. So SP. L and W read: ". . . and the day of death is secret, and the day when the King Messiah will come is secret," etc.

90. So SP. W reads: "May His kingdom be magnified over us."

91. So SP. W reads "Greece."

92. Because of the euphony, this was probably vocalized עֲנָנִי *Anani* and may have been the source of the present Targumic rendering. However, the Talmud is unvocalized, so the vocalization of Daniel is here used.

CHAPTER IV

NOTES

1. This conceivably might be the rationale for משיח ישראל of the Qumran literature, though משיח בן אהרון would still constitute a difficulty. The relationship between the Targumic Messianism and that of the Qumranites is yet to be explored.

2. S. H. Levey, "The Date of Targum Jonathan to the Prophets," *Vetus Testamentum*, Vol. XXI, No. 2, April 1971, pp. 186 ff.

APPENDIX

NOTES

1. See discussion, *supra,* p. 36.
2. This might be construed as having the seeds of the Messianic, in view of its reference to "David and his descendants forever," and in the light of the Targumic rendering of 22:28-32 and 23:1 ff., but the Targum simply translates the Hebrew literally.
3. See discussion, *supra,* p. 124.
4. See discussion, *supra,* p. 94.
5. See discussion, *supra,* p. 105.
6. See note 2 above.
7. See discussion, *supra,* pp. 123-124.

BIBLIOGRAPHY

I. Critical Editions of the Targum

Berliner, A. *Targum Onkelos*. Berlin, 1884.

Ginsburger, M. *Das Fragmententhargum*. Berlin, 1884.

―――. *Pseudo-Jonathan*. Berlin, 1903.

Lagarde, Paul de. *Prophetae Chaldaice*. Leipzig, 1872.

―――. *Hagiographa Chaldaice*. Leipzig, 1873.

Macho, A. Diez. *Neophyti I*. 2 vols., Madrid-Barcelona, 1970.

Sperber, Alexander. *The Bible in Aramaic*. 4 vols. Leiden, 1959, 1962, 1968.

II. Other Editions of the Targum

Mikraoth Gedoloth. Pieterkov, 1888.

Mikraoth Gedoloth. Reprint of Warsaw edition, New York, 1951.

III. Rabbinic Sources

Abot de Rabbi Natan. ed. S. Schechter, Vienna, 1887.

Babylonian Talmud. ed. I. Epstein, 18 vols., London, 1961.

Bereshit Rabbah. ed. J. Theodor and H. Albeck, Jerusalem, 1965.

Mekilta. ed. I. H. Weiss, Vienna, 5625.

Mekilta de Rabbi Ishmael. ed. H. S. Horowitz and I. A. Rabin, Frankfurt, 1931.

Mekilta de Rabbi Ishmael. J. Z. Lauterbach, 3 vols. Philadelphia, 1933-35.

Mekilta de Rabbi Shimon b. Johai. ed. J. N. Epstein, Jerusalem, 1955.

Midrash Hagadol. ed. S. Fisch, London, 1957.

Midrash Ha-Gadol. ed. S. Schechter, Cambridge, 1902.

Midrash Rabbah. 2 vols. Wilna, 1878.

Midrash Rabbah. ed. H. Freedman and M. Simon. 10 vols. London, 1951.

Midrash Rabbah. ed. E. E. Ha-Levy, 8 vols., Tel Aviv, 1956-63.

Midrash Tanhuma. ed. S. Buber, New York, 1946.

Midrash Tehillim. ed. S. Buber, Wilna, 1891.

Ozar Midrashim. ed. J. D. Eisenstein, 2 vols., New York, 1915.

Pesikta Rabbati. ed. M. Friedmann, Vienna, 1880.

Pirke de-Rabbi Eliezer. Warsaw, 1852.

Seder Eliyahu Rabba and Seder Eliyahu Zuta. ed. M. Friedmann, Vienna, 1902.

Sifra. ed. L. Finkelstein, New York, 1956.

Sifre. ed. M. Friedmann, Vienna, 5624.

Sifre on Deuteronomy. ed. H. S. Horowitz and I. A. Rabin, Berlin, 1939.

165

Sifre on Numbers. ed. H. S. Horowitz and I. A. Rabin, Leipzig, 1917.
Talmud Babli, 4 vols., Berlin, 5685.
Talmud Babli. 12 vols., Wilna, 1913-14.
Talmud Yerushalmi. Kratoshin, 5626.
Yalkut Shimeoni. Berlin, 1926.

IV. Supplementary Resources

A. Books

Abel, M. *Histoire de la Palestine.* Paris, 1952.
Apocrypha and Pseudepigrapha. ed. R. H. Charles. 2 vols. Oxford, 1913.
Bacher, W. *Die Agada der Tannaiten.* 2 vols. Strassburg, 1884-1890.
————. *Die Agada der palästinischen Amoräer.* 3 vols. Strassburg, 1892-99.
————. *Die Agada der babylonischen Amoräer.* Strassburg, 1878.
————. *Agadot Ha-Tannaim,* etc. 11 vols. tr. A. Z. Rabinowitz, Berlin and Tel Aviv, 1922-35.
Biblia Hebraica. ed. R. Kittel. 2 vols. Leipzig, 1909.
Biblia Sacra Polyglotta. ed. Brian Walton. 6 vols. London, 1657.
Black, M. *An Aramaic Approach to the Gospels and Acts.* Oxford, 1967.
Bokser, B. Z. *Pharisaic Judaism in Transition.* New York, 1935.
Bowker, John. *The Targums and Rabbinic Literature.* Cambridge, 1969.
Braude, W. G. *The Midrash on Psalms.* 2 vols. Yale, 1959.
Briggs, Charles A. *Messianic Prophecy.* New York, 1886.
Churgin, P. *Targum Jonathan to the Prophets.* New Haven, 1927.
————. *Targum Ketuvim.* New York, 1945.
The Complete Bible: An American Translation. Chicago, 1948.
Danielou, J. *The Theology of Jewish Christianity.* tr. J. A. Baker, London, 1964.
Daube, D. *The New Testament and Rabbinic Judaism.* London, 1956.
Davies, W. D. *Torah in the Messianic Age.* Philadelphia, 1952.
————. *Paul and Rabbinic Judaism.* London, 1953.
————. *Christian Origins and Judaism.* London, 1962.
Dialogue with Trypho, Justin Martyr. In *Fathers of the Church.* tr. T. B. Falls, New York, 1949, Vol. VI.
Finkelstein, L. *The Pharisees.* 2 vols. Philadelphia, 1946.
Flusser, D. G. *Megilot Midbar Yehudah.* Jerusalem, 1967.
Goodenough, E. R. *Jewish Symbols in the Greco-Roman Period.* 12 vols. New York, 1953-65.
Goshen-Gottstein, M. H. *Targume Ha-Mikra Ha-Arami'im.* Jerusalem, 1963.
Graetz, H. *History of the Jews.* Philadelphia, 1895.
Gray, G. B. *A Critical and Exegetical Commentary on the Book of Isaiah,* New York, 1912.
Greenstone, J. H. *The Messiah Idea in Jewish History.* Philadelphia, 1906.

Gressmann, H. *Der Messias.* Goettingen, 1929.
Guttmann, A. *Rabbinic Judaism in the Making.* Detroit, 1970.
The Holy Bible. Confraternity-Downy version, New York, 1954.
The Holy Bible. Revised Standard Version. New York, 1953.
The Holy Scriptures, According to the Masoretic Text. Philadelphia, 1943.
Hooke, S. H. *Judaism and Christianity.* ed. W. O. E. Oesterly. New York, 1937.
Jastrow, Marcus. *A Dictionary of the Targumim, the Talmud Babli and Yerushalmi, and the Midrashic Literature.* 2 vols. London, 1903.
Kaufmann, J. *Midrashe Geulah.* Jerusalem, 1954.
Klausner, J. *Hara'yon Hameshihi Beyisrael.* Tel Aviv, 5710.
Lauterbach, J. Z. *Rabbinic Essays.* Cincinnati, 1951.
Levy, J. J. *Chaldäisches Wörterbuch über die Targumim.* Leipzig, 1876.
Mc Namara, M. *The New Testament and the Palestinian Targum to the Pentateuch.* Rome, 1966.
Moore, G. F. *Judaism in the First Centuries of the Christian Era, the Age of the Tannaim.* 3 vols. Cambridge, 1927.
Mowinckel, S. *He That Cometh,* tr. G. W. Anderson. New York, 1954.
Neusner, J. *A Life of Rabban Yohanan ben Zakkai.* Leiden, 1962.
Nickels, P. *Targum and New Testament, a Bibliography.* Rome, 1967.
Oesterley, W. O. E. *The Evolution of the Messianic Idea.* New York, 1909.
Sarachek, J. *The Doctrine of the Messiah in Medieval Jewish Literature.* New York, 1932.
Schechter, S. *Aspects of Rabbinic Theology.* New York, 1909.
Scholem, G. *The Messianic Idea in Judaism.* New York, 1971.
The Septuagint Version of the Old Testament. London, n.d.
The Shepherd of Hermas. In *The Apostolic Fathers,* tr. E. J. Goodspeed. New York, 1950.
Silver, A. H. *A History of Messianic Speculation in Israel from the First through the Seventeenth Centuries.* New York, 1927.
Skinner, J. *A Critical and Exegetical Commentary on Genesis.* New York, 1910.
Stenning, J. F. *The Targum of Isaiah.* Oxford, 1949.
Vermes, G. *Scripture and Tradition in Judaism.* Leiden, 1961.
Weinberg, J. *L'Tol'dot Ha-Targumim.* New York, 1964.
Young, R. *Christology of the Targums.* Edinburgh, n.d.
Zeitlin, S. *The Rise and Fall of the Judean State.* 2 vols. Philadelphia, 1967
Zunz, L. *Die gottesdienstlichen Vorträge der Juden.* Frankfurt, 1892.

B. Articles
Bacher, W. "Targum." *The Jewish Encyclopedia,* XII, 1906.
Buttenwieser, M. "Messiah." *The Jewish Encyclopedia,* VIII, 1904.
Emmet, C. W. "Messiah." *Encyclopaedia of Religion and Ethics,* ed. James Hastings. VIII, 1928.

Ginsberg, H. L., et al. "Messiah." *Encyclopaedia Judaica,* XI, 1971.

Ginzberg, L. "Armilus." *The Jewish Encyclopedia,* II, 1903.

Gressmann, H. "The Sources of Israel's Messianic Hope." *American Journal of Theology,* XVII (April, 1913), 173-194.

Grutzmacher, G. "Jerome." *Encyclopaedia of Religion and Ethics,* ed. James Hastings. VII, 1904.

Hirschberg, H. "Eighteen Hundred Years Before Freud: A Re-Evaluation of the Term Yetzer Ha-Ra." *Judaism,* X (Spring, 1961), 129-41.

Klatzkin, J. "Armilus." *Encyclopaedia Judaica,* II, 1971.

Klausner, J.; Hartmann, L. F.; and Scholem, G. "Eschatology." *Encyclopaedia Judaica,* VI, 1971.

Kohler, K. "Eschatology." *The Jewish Encyclopedia,* V, 1903.

Krauss, S. "Jerome." *The Jewish Encyclopedia,* VII, 1904.

Levey, S. H. "The Date of Targum Jonathan to the Prophets." *Vetus Testamentum,* XXI (April, 1971), 186 ff.

————. "The Targum to the Book of Ruth: Its Linguistic and Exegetical Character." Unpublished Rabbinical Thesis, Hebrew Union College, Cincinnati, 1934.

Lowe, R. "Apologetic Motifs in the Targum to the Song of Songs." *Biblical Motifs,* ed. A. Altmann, Cambridge, 1966.

Rhine, A. "Chosroes II." *Jewish Encyclopedia,* IV, 1903.

Smith, H. P. "Origin of the Messianic Hope in Israel." *American Journal of Theology,* XIV (July, 1910), 337-360.

SCRIPTURAL PASSAGES AND TARGUM

* Indicates no Targumic rendering

INDEX II

INTERTESTAMENTAL LITERATURE AND NEW TESTAMENT

RABBINIC REFERENCES

TALMUD

MIDRASH

GENERAL INDEX

INDEX V

MODERN AUTHORITIES